500 RECIPES FOR
COCKTAILS AND MIXED DRINKS

500 RECIPES
FOR COCKTAILS
AND MIXED DRINKS

By Felix Brenner

HAMLYN
LONDON · NEW YORK · SYDNEY · TORONTO

Cover photograph by Paul Williams

Published by The Hamlyn Publishing Group Limited
London · New York · Sydney · Toronto
Astronaut House, Feltham, Middlesex, England

Fifteenth impression 1981

ISBN 0 600 03421 6

Printed and bound in Great Britain by
Morrison & Gibb Ltd., London and Edinburgh

Contents

Introduction

When are mixed drinks served? The occasions are so many that it is easier to say that the only time mixed drinks are not served is during a meal.

At any other time there are mixed drinks to serve the purpose. They can be used as an aperitif to stimulate the appetite; be relaxing served after a meal and, for sheer conviviality, there are few institutions like the friendly cocktail party.

Mix a drink just for yourself, to unwind when you come home from a day's work, or quietly sip a drink while reading or watching the television.

The varieties of mixed drinks are unlimited. As you become more familiar with the ingredients, the techniques and the flavour and bouquet combinations, your scope and inventiveness in making mixed drinks will grow. The possibility of combinations depends solely on what you have available in your cupboard. Even the simplest and most economical stock of ingredients has numerous possibilities.

In this book you will find all the 'standard' mixes, those universally popular drinks whose names and contents are essentially the same in every country of the world: the Dry Martini Cocktail, the Old-Fashioned, the Collinses, and so on. Here, too, is a wide ranging variety of 'local' drinks from all parts of the globe, to add an easily achieved touch of the exotic.

Most important of all, perhaps, you'll find recipes for basic mixed drinks and ideas from which, with experience and ingenuity you will be able to contrive your own variations.

Much has been said and written about the 'mystique' of making and serving mixed drinks. There are those who maintain it is unforgiveable to defile whisky and soda with ice. There are some people who swear that fresh spring water is whisky's only true mate. And do not forget the die-hard who will be shocked by the idea of anything being mixed with whisky. Some people, spoiled by a bit of tropical life, will not touch a rum punch that has not been made with any but the freshest of fruits.

Obviously there is not a bar or an hotel anywhere in the world that can furnish in a trice all the ideal ingredients of every drink the whole year round; certainly the households are few that could afford them.

The contents of your mixed drinks depend very largely on the range of your pocket, the availability of ideal ingredients and, above all, your own taste. Drinks are intended to give pleasure to the drinker. If someone likes his whisky best when frozen nearly solid and flooded with bitter lemon, let him drink it that way. Mix your drink your way and let the purist rage.

A well-mixed drink will taste good no matter in what glass it is served. The costliest goblet

will not improve the flavour of a badly made drink. Custom has decreed, not forcibly, that some drinks are more appropriately served in certain shapes of glasses. This is generally because of the size and mixture of the drink. An ordinary wine glass however will serve perfectly and handsomely for any drink.

If you have the variety of shapes at your command you will find the recipes here will suggest the glass in which the drink is usually served.

These shapes are: The Collins glass for Collins, Lemonade, Rickeys, etc.

The Highball glass for Cuba Librés, Fizzes, Highballs, etc.

The Lowball glass for Americanos, Frappées, Rum Punches, etc.

The Old-Fashioned glass for Old-Fashioneds, Sazeracs, Mists, etc.

The Champagne glass for Champagne cocktails, Frozen Daiquiris, etc.

The Martini glass for Manhattans, Martini cocktails, Perfects, etc.

The Sour glass for Alexanders, Sours, etc.

Almost all mixed drinks taste better when served ice cold. Therefore you will find it wise to provide yourself with a good supply of ice when you entertain. It is also wise to chill your glasses until you are ready to fill them. One of the few exceptions to this is whisky when served with soda or water, and brandy when served after dinner with soda or water.

There are two types of containers in which you can best mix your drinks. Those that are to be stirred are best prepared in a tall glass jug, with a wide opening, but a tightly curled pouring lip. Those drinks that are to be shaken are best prepared in a shaker made of two wide-topped cylinders of nearly equal size, one metal and the other glass.

The ingredients are put in the glass half, with the ice in it, then the metal half placed on top. Holding each half, the metal cylinder on top, in the left hand, and the glass in the right hand the cocktail is vigorously shaken up and down. Put the shaker down, glass on the bottom, and with a gentle tap the metal top will release itself. If you have this type of shaker, commonly used in bars, you will find that, with a bar strainer, the glass half with serve equally well for the preparation of stirred cocktails.

If your cocktail shaker has a tight fitting metal cap you may find it sticking to the glass part, but keep your hand dry and warm and the top will be more easily released. A plastic lipped

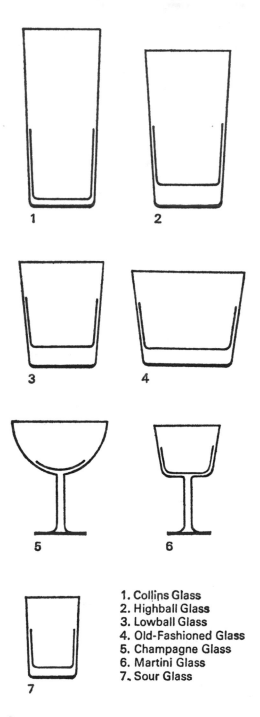

1. Collins Glass
2. Highball Glass
3. Lowball Glass
4. Old-Fashioned Glass
5. Champagne Glass
6. Martini Glass
7. Sour Glass

jug with lid can be used if you do not have a cocktail shaker.

Other useful bar equipment and gadgets are a bar strainer, a long handled metal spoon, a corkscrew, bottle opener, a lemon squeezer and a small sharp fruit knife.

In the recipes the word 'part' is to be read as an indefinite unit of measure, the size or amount of which can vary according to personal taste. In this book a part is represented as consisting of 1–1¼ fl.oz. (approximately 1½–2 tablespoons). The most widely used spirits in mixed drinks are gin, rum, vodka, whisky and brandy. Most cocktails call for at least one of the following ingredients, bitters, French (dry) vermouth, Italian (sweet) vermouth, grenadine, sugar, lemon, orange, grapefruit and occasionally pineapple juice. Long drinks are most frequently diluted with soda, dry ginger-ale, ginger beer or just plain ice water. Some cocktails call for liqueurs such as Bénédictine, Crême de Cacao, Cointreau, Curaçao, Drambuie, Crême de Menthe or Pernod.

With at least some of this equipment and some of these ingredients and this book to guide and inspire you, your future as a barman-host should be bright and enjoyable, for yourself and your guests. Cheers!

Gin Drinks

There are several kinds of gin, not all of them equally useful in making mixed drinks, and certainly not all alike in flavour. The ordinary gin, known in the United States as Dry or London dry gin, is the most commonly used.

Tom gin is a slightly more perfumed and a sweeter gin; Golden gin is somewhere between the two. Plymouth gin is the driest of all, and the sweetest is Sloe gin. Dutch gin is not really meant for mixed drinks.

Long drinks that are stirred

Gin and Lime
you will need for 1 glass:

2–3 ice cubes	1½ parts bottled lime juice
1 part gin	2–2½ parts cold water

1 Place the ice cubes into a highball glass.
2 Pour in the lime juice and gin.
3 Add the water.
4 Stir and serve.

Gin and Tonic
you will need for 1 glass:

2–3 ice cubes	2–2½ parts tonic water
1 part gin	1 slice lemon

1 Place ice cubes into a highball glass.
2 Pour the gin and tonic water over the ice.
3 Garnish with a slice of lemon.
4 Stir and serve.

Note
Some people prefer the additional flavour obtained when the lemon slice is put in before the liquids.

Gin and Ginger
you will need for 1 glass:

2–3 ice cubes	1 slice fresh lemon
1 part gin	1 sprig fresh mint
2–2½ parts dry ginger ale	(optional)

1 Place ice cubes into a highball glass.
2 Pour in the gin and ginger ale.
3 Garnish with the slice of lemon.
4 Stir gently and add the sprig of mint and serve.

Gin and Coke
you will need for 1 glass:

2–3 ice cubes	2–2½ parts coca cola
1 part gin	1 slice fresh lemon

1 Place the ice cubes in a highball glass.
2 Pour in the gin, followed by the coca cola.
3 Garnish with the slice of lemon.
4 Stir gently and serve.

Salty Dog

you will need for 1 glass:

2-3 ice cubes
pinch salt
1 part gin

2-2½ parts canned
unsweetened
grapefruit juice

1 Put the ice cubes into a highball glass.
2 Put the salt on the ice.
3 Add the gin and grapefruit juice.
4 Stir gently and serve.

Gin and Pineapple

you will need for 1 glass:

2-3 ice cubes
1 part gin

2-2½ parts canned
pineapple juice
1 maraschino cherry

1 Put the ice cubes into a highball glass.
2 Pour in the gin and pineapple juice.
3 Stir gently.
4 Garnish with the cherry and serve.

Orange Blossom

you will need for 1 glass:

2-3 ice cubes
1-2 drops Angostura
  bitters
1 part gin

2 parts fresh or
  unsweetened canned
  orange juice
1 sprig fresh mint
  (optional)

1 Put the ice cubes into a highball glass.
2 Shake the Angostura bitters on to the ice cubes.
3 Add the gin and orange juice.
4 Stir gently.
5 Garnish with the fresh mint and serve.

Gin Rickey

you will need for 1 glass:

3-4 ice cubes
½ teaspoon sugar or
  sugar syrup
juice 1 fresh lime

3 parts gin
soda water
1 maraschino cherry
1 sprig fresh mint

1 Put the ice cubes into a highball glass.
2 Put the sugar over the ice and add the fruit juice and gin.
3 Stir evenly to allow the sugar to melt.
4 Spray the soda into the glass.
5 Add the maraschino cherry.
6 Garnish with the mint and serve.

Gin Cooler

you will need for 1 glass:

3-4 ice cubes
½ teaspoon grenadine
juice 1 fresh lemon
3 parts gin

soda water
1 maraschino cherry
1 slice fresh lemon

1 Put the ice cubes into a highball glass.
2 Pour the grenadine over the ice, then the lemon juice and gin.
3 Stir evenly allowing the mixture to blend thoroughly.
4 Top with the soda water.
5 Add the maraschino cherry.
6 Garnish with the lemon and serve.

Southern Gin Cooler

you will need for 1 glass:

3-4 ice cubes
½ teaspoon sugar or
  sugar syrup
juice 1 fresh lemon

3 parts gin
soda water
1 slice fresh lemon
1 sprig fresh mint

1 Put the ice cubes into a highball glass.
2 Put the sugar, fruit juice and gin over the ice.
3 Stir thoroughly to mix the liquids.
4 Top with soda water.
5 Garnish with lemon and mint and serve.

Short drinks that are stirred

Gin and French

you will need for 1 glass:

½ measure dry French 1 measure gin
  vermouth

1 Pour vermouth and gin into a sherry glass.
2 Stir very gently, once or twice, and serve.

Pink Gin

you will need for 1 glass:

dash Angostura bitters 2–2½ parts ice cold water
1 part gin

1 Put the dash of bitters into a sour glass.
2 Swill the liquid around the glass until it spreads along the sides.
3 Add the gin, followed by the ice cold water and serve.

Gin and Italian

you will need for 1 glass:

½ measure sweet Italian 1 measure gin
  vermouth

1 Pour vermouth and gin into a sherry glass.
2 Stir very gently, once or twice, and serve.

Cornwell

you will need for 1 glass:

2 drops orange bitters ice cold water (optional)
1 part gin

1 Put the orange bitters into a sherry glass.
2 Swill these around so that they cling to the sides.
3 Add the gin, and if wanted a little ice cold water.

Dry Martini Cocktails

Although these are very easily prepared drinks there are more theories and rituals about the proper method of preparation than almost any other cocktail. Also there are innumerable variations. The one commonly agreed essential is that they must be served ice cold.

Dry Martini Cocktail

you will need for 1 glass:

5–6 ice cubes   3 parts gin
1 part dry French   1 Spanish olive
  vermouth

1 Put the ice cubes into a glass jug.
2 Pour the vermouth and gin over the ice.
3 Stir (never shake) vigorously and evenly without splashing.
4 Strain and pour into a chilled martini glass.
5 Spear the olive with a toothpick and drop it into the drink.

Very Dry Martini Cocktail

you will need for 1 glass:

5–6 ice cubes   4 parts gin
1 part dry French   1 slice fresh lemon rind
  vermouth

1 Put the ice cubes into a glass jug.
2 Pour the vermouth and gin over the ice.
3 Stir (never shake) vigorously and evenly without splashing.
4 Strain and pour into a chilled martini glass.
5 Twist the lemon rind over the drink and drop it in.

Pink Gilbey

you will need for 1 glass:

5–6 ice cubes   1 part Chamberyzette
2 drops Angostura   4 parts gin
  bitters   1 slice fresh lemon rind

1 Put the ice cubes into a glass jug.
2 Shake the bitters over the ice.
3 Pour in the Chamberyzette and gin.
4 Stir (never shake) vigorously and evenly without splashing.
5 Rub the lemon rind gently around the edge of the chilled martini glass.
6 Strain and pour the mixture into the glass.
7 Twist the lemon rind over the drink and drop it in.

Extra Dry Martini Cocktail

you will need for 1 glass:

5–6 ice cubes
1 part dry French vermouth
5 parts gin
1 pickled pearl onion

1 Put the ice cubes into a glass jug.
2 Pour the vermouth and gin over the ice.
3 Stir (never shake) vigorously and evenly without splashing.
4 Strain and pour the mixture into a chilled martini glass.
5 Spear a pickled onion and drop it in the drink.

Variation

With an olive: Substitute the onion with an olive stuffed with anchovy.

New Orleans Dry Martini Cocktail

you will need for 1 glass:

5–6 ice cubes
2–3 drops Pernod
1 part dry French vermouth
4 parts gin

1 Put the ice cubes into a glass jug.
2 Pour the Pernod over the ice.
3 Pour in the vermouth and gin.
4 Stir (never shake) vigorously and evenly without splashing.
5 Strain and pour into a chilled martini glass.

Gibson (the original recipe)

you will need for 1 glass:

5–6 ice cubes
1 part extra dry sherry
5 parts gin
1 pickled pearl onion

1 Put the ice cubes into a glass jug.
2 Pour the sherry and gin over the ice.
3 Stir (never shake) vigorously and evenly without splashing.
4 Strain and pour into a chilled martini glass.
5 Spear an onion with a toothpick, drop it into the drink and serve.

Gin Perfect

you will need for 1 glass:

5–6 ice cubes
1 part dry French vermouth
1 part sweet Italian vermouth
3 parts gin
1 slice fresh lemon rind

1 Put the ice cubes into a glass jug.
2 Pour the vermouths and gin over the ice.
3 Stir (never shake) vigorously and evenly without splashing.
4 Rub the lemon rind gently around the rim of a chilled martini glass.
5 Strain and pour the mixture into the glass.
6 Twist the lemon rind over the drink and drop it into the glass.

Rosington

you will need for 1 glass:

5–6 ice cubes
1 part Italian (sweet) vermouth
3 parts gin
1 slice fresh orange rind

1 Put the ice cubes into a glass jug.
2 Pour the vermouth and gin over the ice.
3 Stir (never shake) vigorously and evenly without splashing.
4 Strain and pour into a chilled martini glass.
5 Twist the orange rind over the drink and drop it in.

Gimlet

you will need for 1 glass:

5–6 ice cubes
1 part bottled lime juice
3 parts gin

1 Put the ice cubes into a glass jug.
2 Pour in the lime juice and gin.
3 Stir (never shake) vigorously and evenly without splashing.
4 Strain and pour into a chilled martini glass.

Dubonnet Cocktail

you will need for 1 glass:

5–6 ice cubes	1 part gin
1 part Dubonnet	1 slice fresh lemon rind

1 Pour the ice cubes into a glass jug.
2 Pour the Dubonnet and gin over the ice.
3 Stir vigorously, without splashing.
4 Strain and pour into a chilled martini glass.
5 Twist the fresh lemon rind over the mixture, drop it in and serve.

Zaza

you will need for 1 glass:

5–6 ice cubes	1 part Dubonnet
3 drops orange bitters	2 parts gin

1 Put the ice cubes into a glass jug.
2 Shake the orange bitters over the ice.
3 Add the Dubonnet and gin.
4 Stir vigorously without splashing.
5 Strain and pour into a chilled martini glass.

Long drinks that are shaken

Wherever sugar is called for, it is advisable to use sugar syrup (see Glossary) as it gives more 'body' to the drink.

John Collins
(Tom Collins in U.S.A.)

you will need for 1 glass:

5–6 ice cubes	3 parts gin
1 teaspoon sugar or sugar syrup	1 slice fresh lemon
	1 sprig fresh mint
1 part fresh lemon juice	soda water

1 Put the ice cubes into a cocktail shaker.
2 Pour in the sugar, lemon juice and gin.
3 Shake vigorously until a frost forms.
4 Pour without straining into a collins glass.
5 Garnish with the lemon and mint.
6 Top with soda water, stir gently and serve.

Sydney Fizz

you will need for 1 glass:

4–5 ice cubes	½ teaspoon grenadine
1 part fresh lemon juice	3 parts gin
1 part fresh orange juice (or canned, unsweetened)	soda water

1 Put the ice cubes into a cocktail shaker.
2 Pour the fruit juices, grenadine and gin over the ice.
3 Shake vigorously until a frost forms.
4 Strain and pour into a lowball glass.
5 Top with soda and serve.

Ramos Gin Fizz

you will need for 1 glass:

1 egg white	3 parts gin
4–5 ice cubes	3 drops Angostura
1 part fresh lemon juice	bitters
1 part thin cream	soda water (optional)

1 Put the ice cubes into a cocktail shaker.
2 Pour in the lemon juice, cream and gin.
3 Add the egg white to the gin mixture.
4 Put Angostura bitters over the mixture.
5 Shake until a frost forms.
6 Pour without straining into a highball glass; if wanted top with soda water, and serve.

Morning Glory Fizz

you will need for 1 glass:

4–5 ice cubes	3 parts gin
1 part fresh lemon juice	1 egg white
½ teaspoon sugar or sugar syrup	3 drops Pernod
	ginger ale

1 Put the ice cubes into a cocktail shaker.
2 Pour the lemon juice, sugar and gin over the ice.
3 Add the egg white to the gin mixture.
4 Add the Pernod.
5 Shake until a frost forms.
6 Strain and pour into a lowball glass and top with ginger ale.

Silver Fizz

you will need for 1 glass:

4–5 ice cubes
½ teaspoon sugar or
  sugar syrup

1 part fresh lemon juice
3 parts gin
1 egg white
soda water

1 Put the ice cubes into a cocktail shaker.
2 Pour the sugar, lemon juice and gin over the ice.
3 ...the egg white to the mixture.
4
5
6

Gin Floradora

you will need for 1 glass:

4–5 ice cubes
½ teaspoon sugar or
  sugar syrup
juice ½ fresh lime

½ teaspoon grenadine
2 parts gin
dry ginger ale

1 Put the ice cubes into a cocktail shaker.
2 Pour in the sugar, lime juice, grenadine and gin.
3 Shake until a frost forms.
...g into a highball glass.
...le and serve.

...glass:

3 parts gin
soda water

...o a cocktail shaker.
..., cherry brandy and gin over

...orms.
...ng into a highball glass.
...r and serve.

...in Sling

...glass:

3 drops Angostura
  bitters
...e (or 1 slice fresh orange
...ned, 1 slice fresh lemon
...e) 1 maraschino cherry
  (optional)
soda water

...nto a cocktail shaker.
...s, cherry brandy and gin.
...r the mixture.
... until a frost forms.
...es into a collins glass.
...out straining into glass.
...slices of fruit.
...y.
...ter and serve.

Authentic rough-crushed guacamole

Serves: 6-8
Preparation time: 10 minutes

3 ripe avocados
½ white or red onion, peeled
  and finely chopped
1 small green chilli, deseeded
  and finely chopped
1 large clove garlic, peeled
  and crushed
Juice of 1 lime
1 tbsp olive oil
Salt and freshly ground
  black pepper

2 tomatoes, deseeded and
  finely chopped
15g fresh coriander, roughly
  chopped
1 bag of tortilla chips, to serve

Halve the avocados, remove the stones, and scoop the flesh into a large bowl, removing any black bits. Mash with a balloon whisk or fork until you have a chunky paste. Add the finely chopped onion, chilli, crushed garlic, lime juice and olive oil, and mix well.

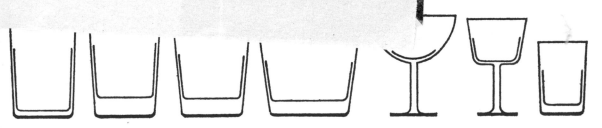

Short drinks that are shaken

Deacon

you will need for 1 glass:

4–5 ice cubes
½ teaspoon sugar or sugar syrup
1 part fresh grapefruit juice (or canned, unsweetened)
3 parts gin

1 Put the ice cubes into a cocktail shaker.
2 Pour in the sugar, fruit juice and gin.
3 Shake until a frost forms, strain and pour into a chilled martini glass.

Gin Sour

you will need for 1 glass:

4–5 ice cubes
1 part fresh lemon juice
½ teaspoon sugar or sugar syrup
3 parts gin
1 maraschino cherry (optional)

1 Put the ice cubes into a cocktail shaker.
2 Pour the lemon juice, sugar and gin over the ice.
3 Shake until a frost forms.
4 Strain and pour into a sour glass; drop in the cherry and serve.

Bronx

you will need for 1 glass:

4–5 ice cubes
1 part dry French vermouth
1 part sweet Italian vermouth
½ part fresh or unsweetened canned orange juice
3 parts gin

1 Put the ice cubes into a cocktail shaker.
2 Pour the vermouths, orange juice and gin over the ice.
3 Shake vigorously, strain and pour into a chilled martini glass.

Haberfield

you will need for 1 glass:

4–5 ice cubes
1 part fresh lemon juice
1 part dry French vermouth
3 parts gin

1 Put the ice cubes into a cocktail shaker.
2 Pour the lemon juice, vermouth and gin over the ice.
3 Shake vigorously, strain and pour into a chilled martini glass.

Outback

you will need for 1 glass:

4–5 ice cubes
1 part dry French vermouth
1 part cherry brandy
3 parts gin

1 Put the ice cubes into a cocktail shaker.
2 Pour the vermouth, cherry brandy and gin over the ice.
3 Shake vigorously, strain and pour into a chilled martini glass.

Bondi

you will need for 1 glass:

4–5 ice cubes
juice ½ fresh lemon
juice 1 fresh orange (or 4 tablespoons canned unsweetened juice)
½ part grenadine
1 part sweet Italian vermouth
3 parts gin

1 Put the ice cubes into a cocktail shaker.
2 Pour the fruit juices, grenadine, vermouth and gin over the ice.
3 Shake vigorously, until a frost forms.
4 Strain and pour into a sour glass.

Honolulu

you will need for 1 glass:

4–5 ice cubes
1 part pineapple juice
1 part fresh lemon juice
1 part fresh orange juice (or canned, unsweetened)
½ teaspoon grenadine
3 parts gin

1 Put the ice cubes into a cocktail shaker.
2 Pour the fruit juices, grenadine and gin over the ice.
3 Shake until a frost forms.
4 Strain and pour into a sour glass.

Waikiki

you will need for 1 glass:

4–5 ice cubes
1 part pineapple juice
1 part fresh lemon juice
½ part dry French vermouth
3 parts gin

1 Put the ice cubes into a cocktail shaker.
2 Pour the fruit juices, vermouth and gin over the ice.
3 Shake until a frost forms.
4 Strain and pour into a sour glass.

Mumu

you will need for 1 glass:

4–5 ice cubes
1 part pineapple juice
1 part fresh grapefruit juice (or canned, unsweetened)
1 teaspoon sugar or sugar syrup
3 parts gin
1 maraschino cherry (optional)

1 Pour the ice cubes into a cocktail shaker.
2 Pour the fruit juices, sugar and gin over the ice.
3 Shake until a frost forms.
4 Strain and pour into a sour glass, drop in the cherry and serve.

Clover Club

you will need for 1 glass:

1 egg white
4–5 ice cubes
juice 1 fresh lime
½ teaspoon sugar or sugar syrup
3 parts gin

1 Put the ice cubes into a cocktail shaker.
2 Pour the lime juice, sugar, egg white, and gin over the ice.
3 Shake until a frost forms.
4 Strain and pour into a sour glass.

Pink Clover Club

you will need for 1 glass:

1 egg white
4–5 ice cubes
juice 1 fresh lime
5 drops grenadine
3 parts gin

1 Put the ice cubes into a cocktail shaker.
2 Pour the lime juice, the grenadine, egg white and gin over the ice.
3 Shake until frost forms, strain and pour into a sour glass.

Johnny-from-London

you will need for 1 glass:

4–5 ice cubes
juice 1 fresh lemon
1 part kirsch
3 parts gin
2 drops Angostura bitters
about 1 teaspoon port

1 Put the ice cubes into a cocktail shaker.
2 Pour the lemon juice, kirsch and gin over the ice.
3 Dash the bitters into the mixture.
4 Shake until frost forms, strain and pour into a sour glass.
5 Top with the port and serve.

Exotic cocktails

Gin Sazerac

you will need for 1 glass:

1 cube lump sugar
2 drops Angostura bitters
about 4 drops Pernod
2–3 ice cubes
gin
1 slice fresh lemon rind

1 Put the lump sugar into an old-fashioned glass.
2 Pour the bitters on to the sugar.
3 Add the Pernod and swill the mixture around the glass.
4 Put in the ice cubes and pour the gin over the ice.
5 Stir gently, squeeze the lemon rind over the drink and serve.

Asylum

you will need for 1 glass:

2–3 ice cubes
3 drops grenadine
1 part Pernod
1 part gin

1 Put the ice cubes into an old-fashioned glass.
2 Put the grenadine over the ice.
3 Add the Pernod and gin.
4 Stir gently and serve.

Delmonico

you will need for 1 glass:

3–4 ice cubes
2–3 drops Angostura bitters
1 part dry French vermouth
1 part sweet Italian vermouth
1 part brandy
2 parts gin
1 slice fresh lemon rind

1 Put the ice cubes into a glass jug.
2 Put the bitters over the ice.
3 Pour in the vermouths, brandy and gin.
4 Stir evenly, without splashing, strain and pour into a chilled martini glass.
5 Twist the lemon rind over the mixture and drop it in.

Negroni

you will need for 1 glass:

2–3 ice cubes
½ part Campari bitters
1 part sweet Italian vermouth
2 parts gin
1 slice fresh orange
soda water

1 Put the ice cubes into a lowball glass.
2 Pour the Campari bitters, vermouth and gin over the ice.
3 Garnish with a slice of orange and top with soda water.

Adelaide

you will need for 1 glass:

4–5 ice cubes
Juice ¼ fresh lime
1 part sweet Italian vermouth
2 parts gin
½ teaspoon grenadine

1 Put the ice cubes into a glass jug.
2 Pour the lime juice, vermouth and gin over the ice.
3 Add the grenadine.
4 Stir gently, strain and pour into a chilled martini glass.

Sea Breeze

you will need for 1 glass:

4–5 ice cubes
1 part fresh grapefruit juice (or canned, unsweetened)
1 part dry French vermouth
3 parts gin

1 Put the ice cubes into a glass jug.
2 Pour the grapefruit juice, vermouth and gin over the ice.
3 Stir gently, strain and pour into a chilled martini glass.

Betty Mac

you will need for 1 glass:

3–4 ice cubes
½ part Amer Picon
1 part sweet Italian vermouth
2 parts gin
½ teaspoon grenadine
1 slice fresh orange

1 Put the ice cubes into a lowball glass.
2 Pour in the Amer Picon, vermouth and gin.
3 Add the grenadine and stir gently.
4 Garnish with a slice of orange and serve.

King Cocktail

you will need for 1 glass:

4–5 ice cubes
2–3 drops orange bitters
2–3 drops Angostura bitters
1 part sweet Italian vermouth
2 parts gin

1 Put the ice cubes into a glass jug.
2 Put the orange and Angostura bitters over the ice.
3 Add the vermouth and gin.
4 Stir evenly, strain and pour into a chilled martini glass.

Poet's Dream

you will need for 1 glass:

4–5 ice cubes
1 part Bénédictine
1 part dry French vermouth
3 parts gin
1 slice fresh lemon rind

1 Put the ice cubes into a glass jug.
2 Pour the Bénédictine, vermouth and gin over the ice.
3 Stir vigorously, without splashing.
4 Strain and pour into a chilled martini glass.
5 Twist the fresh lemon rind over the mixture, drop lemon rind into it and serve.

Opera

you will need for 1 glass:

4–5 ice cubes
1 part Dubonnet
½ part Curaçao
2 parts gin

1 Put the ice cubes into a glass jug.
2 Pour the Dubonnet, Curaçao and gin over the ice.
3 Stir evenly, strain and pour into a chilled martini glass.

San Martin

you will need for 1 glass:

4–5 ice cubes
2 drops Angostura bitters
3 drops Pernod
1 part dry French vermouth
1 part sweet Italian vermouth
2 parts gin

1 Put the ice cubes into a glass jug.
2 Put the Angostura bitters over the ice.
3 Add the Pernod, the vermouths and gin.
4 Stir vigorously, without splashing, strain and pour into a chilled martini glass.

Swan

you will need for 1 glass:

4–5 ice cubes
juice 1 fresh lime
3 drops Pernod
2 drops Angostura bitters
1 part dry French vermouth
2 parts gin

1 Put the ice cubes into a glass jug.
2 Pour in the lime juice.
3 Put the Pernod and the bitters over the ice.
4 Add the vermouth and gin.
5 Stir vigorously, without splashing, strain and pour into a chilled martini glass.

Union League

you will need for 1 glass:

4–5 ice cubes
3 drops orange bitters
1 part port
2 parts gin

1 Put the ice cubes into a glass jug.
2 Put the orange bitters over the ice.
3 Pour in the port and gin.
4 Stir evenly, strain and pour into a chilled martini glass.

Jo'burg

you will need for 1 glass:

4–5 Ice cubes
2–3 drops Angostura bitters
¼ teaspoon white Curaçao
1 part dry French vermouth
1 part sweet Italian vermouth
2 parts gin

1 Put the ice cubes into a glass jug.
2 Put the bitters over the ice.
3 Add the Curaçao, the vermouths and gin.
4 Stir vigorously, strain and pour into a chilled martini glass.

United Services

you will need for 1 glass:

4–5 ice cubes
juice ½ fresh lemon
½ teaspoon white Curaçao
1 part dry French vermouth
2 parts gin

1 Put the ice cubes into a glass jug.
2 Pour the lemon juice, white Curaçao, vermouth and gin over the ice.
3 Stir vigorously, strain and pour into a chilled martini glass.

Blackthorn

you will need for 1 glass:

4–5 ice cubes
2–3 drops Angostura bitters
1 part sweet Italian vermouth
3 parts gin
1 slice fresh lemon rind

1 Put the ice cubes into a glass jug.
2 Put the bitters over the ice.
3 Pour in the vermouth and gin.
4 Stir vigorously, strain and pour into a chilled martini glass.
5 Twist the lemon rind over the drink, drop it in and serve.

19

Pendennis

you will need for 1 glass:

4–5 ice cubes
juice 1 fresh lime or lemon
2–3 drops Peychaud or Angostura bitters
1 part apricot brandy
3 parts gin

1 Put the ice cubes into a glass jug.
2 Pour the fruit juice and the bitters over the ice.
3 Add the apricot brandy and gin.
4 Stir evenly, strain and pour into a chilled martini glass.

Rose

you will need for 1 glass:

4–5 ice cubes
1 part Grand Marnier
3 parts gin

1 Put the ice cubes into a glass jug.
2 Pour the Grand Marnier and gin over the ice.
3 Stir evenly, strain and pour into a chilled martini glass.

Golden Rain

you will need for 1 glass:

4–5 ice cubes
1 part Curaçao
1 part kümmel
2 parts Vielle Curé
3 parts gin

1 Put the ice cubes into a glass jug.
2 Pour the Curaçao, kümmel, Vielle Curé and gin over the ice.
3 Stir evenly, strain and pour into a chilled martini glass.

Sloe Gin Cocktail

you will need for 1 glass:

4–5 ice cubes
2–3 drops orange bitters
1 part gin
2 parts sloe gin

1 Put the ice cubes into a glass jug.
2 Put the bitters over the ice.
3 Pour in the gins, stir vigorously, strain and pour into a chilled martini glass.

Tipperary

you will need for 1 glass:

4–5 ice cubes
juice 1 fresh lemon
1 part dry French vermouth
3 parts sloe gin

1 Put the ice cubes into a glass jug.
2 Pour the lemon juice, vermouth and gin over the ice.
3 Stir evenly, strain and pour into a chilled martini glass.

Macao

you will need for 1 glass:

4–5 ice cubes
3 drops orange bitters
1 part dry French vermouth
1 part sweet Italian vermouth
3 parts sloe gin

1 Put the ice cubes into a glass jug.
2 Put the bitters over the ice.
3 Add the vermouths and gin.
4 Stir evenly, strain and pour into a chilled martini glass.

Gloom Raiser

you will need for 1 glass:

4–5 ice cubes
1 part dry French vermouth
½ teaspoon grenadine
3 drops Pernod
3 parts gin

1 Put the ice cubes into a glass jug.
2 Pour the vermouth, grenadine, Pernod and the gin over the ice.
3 Stir evenly, strain and pour into a chilled martini glass.

Luigi

you will need for 1 glass:

4–5 ice cubes
1 part fresh orange juice
  (or canned,
  unsweetened)
1 part dry French vermouth
½ part Cointreau
1 teaspoon grenadine
2 parts gin

1 Put the ice cubes into a glass jug.
2 Pour the orange juice, vermouth, Cointreau, grenadine and gin over the ice.
3 Stir vigorously, strain and pour into a chilled martini glass.

Monkey's Gland

you will need for 1 glass:

4–5 ice cubes
3 drops Pernod
1 part fresh orange
  juice (or canned,
  unsweetened)
½ teaspoon grenadine
2 parts gin

1 Put the ice cubes into a glass jug.
2 Pour the Pernod, the orange juice, grenadine and gin over the ice.
3 Stir vigorously, strain and pour into a chilled martini glass.

R.A.C.

you will need for 1 glass:

4–5 ice cubes
3 drops orange bitters
1 part dry French
  vermouth
1 part sweet Italian
  vermouth
½ teaspoon grenadine
2 parts gin

1 Put the ice cubes into a glass jug.
2 Put the bitters over the ice.
3 Pour in the vermouths, grenadine and gin.
4 Stir vigorously, strain and pour into a chilled martini glass.

Rambler

you will need for 1 glass:

4–5 ice cubes
1 part dry French
  vermouth
1 part Dubonnet
½ teaspoon grenadine
2 parts gin

1 Put the ice cubes into a glass jug.
2 Pour the vermouths, Dubonnet, grenadine and gin over the ice.
3 Stir vigorously, strain and pour into a chilled martini glass.

Royal

you will need for 1 glass:

4–5 ice cubes
3 drops orange bitters
3 drops Angostura
  bitters
1 part Dubonnet
2 parts gin
1 slice fresh lemon

1 Put the ice cubes into a glass jug.
2 Put the bitters over the ice.
3 Add the Dubonnet and gin.
4 Stir vigorously, strain and pour into a chilled martini glass.
5 Twist the lemon rind over the mixture, drop it in and serve.

Silver

you will need for 1 glass:

4–5 ice cubes
3 drops orange bitters
½ teaspoon maraschino
  or grenadine
1 part dry French
  vermouth
2 parts gin

1 Put the ice cubes into a glass jug.
2 Put the bitters over the ice.
3 Pour in the maraschino, vermouth and gin.
4 Stir vigorously, strain and pour into a chilled martini glass.

Tuxedo

you will need for 1 glass:

4–5 ice cubes
3 drops orange bitters
½ teaspoon grenadine
1 part dry French
  Vermouth
3 parts gin
1 drop Pernod

1 Put the ice cubes into a glass jug.
2 Put the bitters over the ice.
3 Pour in the grenadine, vermouth and gin.
4 Stir vigorously, strain and pour into a chilled martini glass.
5 Add the Pernod to the mixture and serve.

Soso

you will need for 1 glass:

4–5 ice cubes
½ teaspoon grenadine
1 part sweet Italian
  vermouth
1 part Calvados
2 parts gin

1 Put the ice cubes into a glass jug.
2 Pour the grenadine, vermouth, Calvados and gin over the ice.
3 Stir vigorously, strain and pour into a chilled martini glass.

Knockout

you will need for 1 glass:

4–5 ice cubes
1 part dry French
  vermouth

½ part white crème de
  menthe
2 parts gin
1 drop Pernod

1 Put the ice cubes into a glass jug.
2 Pour the vermouth, crème de menthe and gin over the ice.
3 Stir vigorously, strain and pour into a chilled martini glass.
4 Add the Pernod to the mixture and serve.

Cooperstown

you will need for 1 glass:

5–6 ice cubes
1 part dry French
  vermouth
4 parts gin

2 drops white crème de
  menthe
1 sprig fresh mint

1 Put the ice cubes into a glass jug.
2 Pour the vermouth and gin over the ice.
3 Stir thoroughly, without splashing, strain and pour into a chilled martini glass.
4 Add the crème de menthe to the mixture.
5 Garnish with the mint and serve.

Wedding Ball

you will need for 1 glass:

4–5 ice cubes
Juice 1 fresh orange (or
  4 tablespoons canned,
  unsweetened)

1 part Dubonnet
1 part cherry brandy
2 parts gin

1 Put the ice cubes into a glass jug.
2 Pour the orange juice, Dubonnet, brandy and gin over the ice.
3 Stir vigorously, strain and pour into a chilled martini glass.

Xanthia

you will need for 1 glass:

4–5 ice cubes
1 part cherry brandy

1 part yellow Chartreuse
2 parts gin

1 Put the ice cubes into a glass jug.
2 Pour the brandy, Chartreuse and gin over the ice.
3 Stir vigorously, strain and pour into a chilled martini glass.

Boomerang

you will need for 1 glass:

4–5 ice cubes
3 drops Angostura
  bitters
½ teaspoon grenadine

1 part sweet Italian
  vermouth
3 parts gin

1 Put the ice cubes into a glass jug.
2 Put the bitters over the ice.
3 Pour in the grenadine, vermouth and gin.
4 Stir vigorously, strain and pour into a chilled martini glass.

Deep Sea

you will need for 1 glass:

5–6 ice cubes
2 drops Angostura
  bitters
3 drops Pernod

1 part dry French
  vermouth
3 parts gin

1 Put the ice cubes into a glass jug.
2 Put the bitters and the Pernod over the ice.
3 Pour in the vermouth and gin.
4 Stir vigorously, without splashing.
5 Strain and pour into a chilled martini glass.

Dempsey

you will need for 1 glass:

4–5 ice cubes
½ teaspoon grenadine
3 drops Absinthe or Pernod

1 part Calvados
3 parts gin

1 Put the ice cubes into a glass jug.
2 Pour in the grenadine, Pernod, the Calvados and, or Absinthe gin.
3 Stir vigorously, strain and pour into a chilled martini glass.

Diki-diki

you will need for 1 glass:

4–5 ice cubes	1 part Calvados
juice ½ fresh grapefruit	2 parts gin
(or 2½ tablespoons	
canned, unsweetened	
juice)	

1 Put the ice cubes into a cocktail shaker.
2 Pour the grapefruit juice, Calvados and gin over the ice.
3 Shake until a frost forms.
4 Strain and pour into a sour glass.

Golden Dawn

you will need for 1 glass:

4–5 ice cubes	1 part Calvados
Juice ½ fresh orange	1 part apricot brandy
(or 2 tablespoons	3 parts gin
canned, unsweetened	
juice)	

1 Put the ice cubes into a cocktail shaker.
2 Pour the orange juice, Calvados, apricot brandy and gin over the ice.
3 Shake until a frost forms.
4 Strain and pour into a sour glass.

Maiden's Prayer

you will need for 1 glass:

4–5 ice cubes	juice 1 fresh lemon
3 drops Angostura	1 part Cointreau
bitters	2 parts gin

1 Put the ice cubes into a cocktail shaker.
2 Pour the bitters over the ice.
3 Add the lemon juice, Cointreau and gin.
4 Shake until a frost forms.
5 Strain and pour into a sour glass.

Paradise

you will need for 1 glass:

4–5 ice cubes	juice ½ fresh orange
1 teaspoon bottled lime	(or 2 tablespoons
juice	canned, unsweetened
	juice)
	1 part apricot brandy
	3 parts gin

1 Put the ice cubes into a cocktail shaker.
2 Pour the fruit juices, brandy and gin over the ice.
3 Shake until a frost forms.
4 Strain and pour into a sour glass.

Marshall

you will need for 1 glass:

4–5 ice cubes	Cointreau
juice ½ fresh grapefruit	1 part dry French
(or 2½ tablespoons	vermouth
canned, unsweetened	1 part brandy
juice)	3 parts gin

1 Put the ice cubes into a cocktail shaker.
2 Pour the grapefruit juice, Cointreau, vermouth, brandy and gin over the ice.
3 Shake until a frost forms.
4 Strain and pour into a sour glass.

Ranger

you will need for 1 glass:

4–5 ice cubes	1 part dry French
juice ½ fresh grapefruit	vermouth
(or 2½ tablespoons	1 part sweet Italian
canned, unsweetened	vermouth
juice)	½ teaspoon grenadine
	3 parts gin

1 Put the ice cubes into a cocktail shaker.
2 Pour the grapefruit juice, vermouths, grenadine and gin over the ice.
3 Shake until a frost forms.
4 Strain and pour into a glass.

Red Lion

you will need for 1 glass:

4–5 ice cubes	1 part Grand Marnier
juice ½ fresh lemon	2 parts gin
juice ½ fresh orange	
(or 2 tablespoons	
canned, unsweetened	
juice)	

1 Put the ice cubes into a cocktail shaker.
2 Pour the fruit juices, Grand Marnier and gin over the ice.
3 Shake until a frost forms.
4 Strain and pour into a sour glass.

Daisy

you will need for 1 glass:

4–5 ice cubes	juice ½ fresh orange
1 teaspoon raspberry	(or 2 tablespoons
syrup or maraschino	canned, unsweetened
or grenadine	juice)
juice 1 fresh lemon	3 parts gin

1 Put the ice cubes into a cocktail shaker.
2 Pour the syrup, fruit juices and gin over the ice.
3 Shake until a frost forms.
4 Strain and pour into a sour glass.

White Elephant

you will need for 1 glass:

1 egg white
4–5 ice cubes

1 part sweet Italian vermouth
3 parts gin

1 Put the ice cubes into a cocktail shaker.
2 Pour the vermouth, gin and egg white over the ice.
3 Shake until a frost forms.
4 Strain and pour into a sour glass.

Savannah

you will need for 1 glass:

1 egg white
4–5 ice cubes
1 teaspoon crème de cacao

juice ½ fresh orange (or 2 tablespoons canned, unsweetened juice)
2 parts gin

1 Put the ice cubes into a cocktail shaker.
2 Pour the crème de cacao, orange juice and gin over the ice.
3 Add the egg white, shake until a frost forms.
4 Strain and pour into a glass.

Virgin

you will need for 1 glass:

4–5 ice cubes
1 part Forbidden Fruit

1 part white crème de menthe
2 parts gin

1 Put the ice cubes into a cocktail shaker.
2 Pour the Forbidden Fruit, crème de menthe and gin over the ice.
3 Shake until a frost forms.
4 Strain and pour into a chilled martini glass.

Burnsides

you will need for 1 glass:

4–5 ice cubes
2 drops Angostura bitters
1 teaspoon cherry brandy

1 part sweet Italian vermouth
2 parts dry French vermouth
4 parts gin
1 slice fresh lemon rind

1 Put the ice cubes into a cocktail shaker.
2 Put the bitters over the ice.
3 Add the cherry brandy, vermouths and gin.
4 Shake lightly.
5 Strain and pour into a sour glass.
6 Twist the lemon rind over the mixture and drop it in.

Free Silver

you will need for 1 glass:

4–5 ice cubes
juice ½ fresh lemon
1 teaspoon sugar or sugar syrup

1 part white rum
3 parts gin
½ part milk

1 Put the ice cubes into a cocktail shaker.
2 Pour the lemon juice, sugar, rum, gin and milk over the ice.
3 Shake until a frost forms.
4 Strain and pour into a glass.

Au Revoir

you will need for 1 glass :

4–5 ice cubes
juice 1 fresh lemon
1 egg white

1 part brandy
1 part sloe gin

1 Put the ice cubes into a cocktail shaker.
2 Pour the lemon juice, brandy, egg white and sloe gin over the ice.
3 Shake until a frost forms.
4 Strain and pour into a glass.

Long drinks for a heatwave

Cherry Julep

you will need for 1 glass:

3–4 ice cubes
juice ½ fresh lemon
1 teaspoon sugar or
  sugar syrup
1 teaspoon grenadine
1 part cherry brandy
1 part sloe gin
2 parts gin
chopped ice
1 slice fresh lemon
  and/or orange

1 Put the ice cubes into a cocktail shaker.
2 Pour the lemon juice, sugar, grenadine, cherry brandy and gins over the ice.
3 Fill a collins glass with finely chopped ice.
4 Shake the mixture until a frost forms.
5 Strain and pour into the ice-filled glass, garnish with slice of lemon and/or orange.

Gin Cup

(This is best served in a silver mug)

3 sprigs fresh mint
1 teaspoon sugar or
  sugar syrup
chopped ice
juice ½ fresh lemon
3 parts gin

1 Put the mint and sugar into mug.
2 Stir them about, bruising the mint slightly.
3 Fill the mug with chopped ice.
4 Pour the lemon juice and gin into the ice-filled mug.
5 Stir the mixture until a heavy frost starts to form.
6 Wrap a table napkin round the mug and serve.

Frobisher

you will need for 1 glass:

chopped ice
2 drops Angostura
  bitters
3 tablespoons gin
1 slice fresh lemon rind
champagne

1 Fill a highball glass with chopped ice.
2 Shake the bitters on to the ice.
3 Pour in the gin.
4 Squeeze the lemon rind over the drink and drop it into the gin mixture.
5 Fill the glass with champagne and serve.

Gin French '75

you will need for 1 glass:

4–5 ice cubes
juice 1 fresh lime or
  lemon
1 teaspoon sugar or
  sugar syrup
3 parts gin
3 drops Angostura
  bitters
champagne

1 Put the ice cubes into a cocktail shaker.
2 Pour the fruit juice, sugar and gin over the ice.
3 Shake the bitters into the mixture.
4 Shake until a frost forms.
5 Pour without straining into a highball glass.
6 Top with champagne and serve.

Captain's Widow

you will need for 1 glass:

4–5 ice cubes
1 part fresh lemon juice
1 teaspoon sugar or
  sugar syrup
1 part golden rum
4 parts gin
crushed ice

1 Put the ice cubes into a cocktail shaker.
2 Pour the lemon juice, sugar, rum and gin over the ice.
3 Fill a champagne glass with crushed ice.
4 Shake the mixture until a frost forms.
5 Strain and pour into the ice-filled champagne glass.
6 Serve with a drinking straw.

Princess Mary

you will need for 1 glass:

4–5 ice cubes
1 part crème de cacao
1 part thick cream
3 parts gin
cracked ice

1 Put the ice cubes into a cocktail shaker.
2 Pour the crème de cacao, cream and gin over the ice.
3 Fill a sour glass with cracked ice.
4 Shake the mixture until a frost forms.
5 Strain and pour into the ice-filled glass.

Whisky Drinks

That variety of flavour that exists in gin is to be found in the national types of whiskies. Scotch does vary in taste from distiller to distiller, but the great difference lies in the regional brews. Unlike gin there is no similarity of taste between Scotch, Irish, Canadian or the two American whiskies, Rye and Bourbon. With but one exception these spirits are grain distilled: the Brazilian whisky is made from bananas! Most whisky based drinks can employ any one of the types, some however require a specific brew.

Long drinks that are stirred

Whisky and Water

you will need for 1 glass:

2–3 ice cubes   water
1 measure whisky

1 Put the ice cubes into a highball glass.
2 Pour the whisky over the ice.
3 Top with water to taste.

Whisky and Soda

you will need for 1 glass:

2–3 ice cubes   soda
1 measure whisky

1 Put the ice cubes into a high ball glass.
2 Pour the whisky over the ice.
3 Top with soda.

Whisky and Dry Ginger Ale

you will need for 1 glass:

2–3 ice cubes   dry ginger ale
1 measure whisky

1 Put the ice cubes into a highball glass.
2 Pour the whisky over the ice.
3 Top with dry ginger ale.

Whisky Lowball

you will need for 1 glass:

2 ice cubes   water or soda
1 measure whisky

1 Put the ice cubes into a lowball glass.
2 Pour the whisky over the ice.
3 Add a splash of water or soda.

Old-Fashioned

you will need for 1 glass:

1 cube sugar   1 part whisky
2 drops Angostura   1 slice fresh lemon rind
bitters   1 maraschino cherry
2–3 ice cubes   (optional)

1 Put the cube of sugar in the bottom of an old-fashioned glass.
2 Shake the bitters on to the sugar.
3 Mix the sugar and bitters, spreading the mixture around the glass.
4 Put the ice cubes into the glass.
5 Pour the whisky over the ice.
6 Twist the lemon rind over the drink and drop it in.
7 Garnish with the cherry and serve.

Sazerac

you will need for 1 glass:

2–3 ice cubes
1 cube sugar
2 drops Peychaud
  bitters or Angostura
  bitters

2 drops Pernod
bourbon or Scotch
  whisky
1 slice fresh lemon rind

1 Put a cube of sugar in the bottom of an old-fashioned glass.
2 Shake the Peychaud bitters and the Pernod on to the sugar.
3 Swizzle the sugar, bitters and Pernod, spreading the mixture around the glass.
4 Pour the ice cubes into the glass.

5 Pour the whisky over the ice.
6 Stir gently, twist the lemon rind over the drink, drop it in and serve.

Stone

you will need for 1 glass:

2–3 ice cubes
2 parts whisky

cider

1 Put the ice cubes into a highball glass.
2 Add the whisky and cider, stir and serve.

Short drinks that are stirred

Whisky and French

you will need for 1 glass:

1 part dry French
  vermouth

2 parts whisky

1 Pour the vermouth into a sherry glass.
2 Add the whisky.
3 Stir lightly and serve.

Whisky and Italian

you will need for 1 glass:

1 part sweet Italian
  vermouth

2 parts whisky

1 Pour the vermouth into a sherry glass.
2 Add the whisky.
3 Stir lightly and serve.

Cold Toddy

you will need for 1 glass:

2–3 ice cubes
½ teaspoon sugar or
  sugar syrup

water
1 slice fresh lemon rind
2 parts whisky

1 Put the ice cubes into an old-fashioned glass.
2 Pour in the sugar, a little water and the lemon rind.
3 Stir this mixture about.
4 Add the whisky.
5 Stir lightly and serve.

Rob Roy

you will need for 1 glass:

4–5 ice cubes
1 part sweet Italian
  vermouth

3 parts whisky
1 maraschino cherry

1 Put the ice cubes into a glass jug.
2 Pour the vermouth and whisky over the ice.
3 Stir vigorously, strain and pour into a chilled martini glass.
4 Drop in the cherry and serve.

Dry Rob Roy

you will need for 1 glass:

4–5 ice cubes
1 party dry French
  vermouth

3 parts whisky
1 Spanish olive

1 Put the ice cubes into a glass jug.
2 Pour the vermouth and whisky over the ice.
3 Stir vigorously, strain and pour into a chilled martini glass.
4 Drop in the olive and serve.

Manhattan

you will need for 1 glass:

4–5 ice cubes
1 part sweet Italian
  vermouth

3 parts rye or bourbon
1 maraschino cherry

1 Put the ice cubes into a glass jug.
2 Pour the vermouth and whisky over the ice.
3 Stir vigorously, strain and pour into a chilled martini glass.
4 Drop in the cherry and serve.

Whisky Perfect

you will need for 1 glass:

4–5 ice cubes
½ part dry French vermouth
½ part sweet Italian vermouth
3 parts whisky
1 slice fresh lemon rind

1 Put the ice cubes into a glass jug.
2 Pour the vermouths and whisky over the ice.
3 Stir vigorously, strain and pour into a chilled martini glass.
4 Twist the lemon rind over the mixture and drop it in.

Edinburgh

you will need for 1 glass:

4–5 ice cubes
2–3 drops Angostura bitters
½ teaspoon apricot brandy
½ teaspoon crème de menthe
3 parts whisky
1 part dry French vermouth

1 Put the ice cubes into a glass jug.
2 Shake the bitters over the ice.
3 Add the brandy and crème de menthe.
4 Pour the whisky and vermouth over the mixture.
5 Stir vigorously, strain and pour into a chilled martini glass.

Club

you will need for 1 glass:

4–5 ice cubes
3 drops Angostura bitters
½ teaspoon grenadine
3 parts whisky

1 Put the ice cubes into a glass jug.
2 Shake the bitters over the ice.
3 Pour in the grenadine and whisky.
4 Stir vigorously, strain and pour into a chilled martini glass.

Southerly Buster

you will need for 1 glass:

4–5 ice cubes
1 part Curaçao
3 parts whisky
1 slice fresh lemon rind

1 Put the ice cubes into a glass jug.
2 Pour the Curaçao and whisky over the ice.
3 Stir vigorously, strain and pour into a chilled martini glass.
4 Twist the lemon rind over the mixture and drop it in.

The Heather

you will need for 1 glass:

3–4 ice cubes
2–3 drops Angostura bitters
dry French vermouth
2 parts whisky

1 Put the ice cubes into an old-fashioned glass.
2 Shake the bitters over the ice.
3 Add the vermouth and whisky.
4 Stir gently and serve.

Glamis

you will need for 1 glass:

4–6 ice cubes
1 part Drambuie
3 part whisky
1 slice fresh lemon rind

1 Put the ice cubes into a glass jug.
2 Pour the Drambuie and whisky over the ice.
3 Stir vigorously, strain and pour into a chilled martini glass.
4 Twist the lemon rind over the mixture and drop it in.

McKenzie

you will need for 1 glass:

2–3 ice cubes
2–3 drops Angostura bitters
½ teaspoon sugar or sugar syrup
2 parts whisky

1 Put the ice cubes into an old-fashioned glass.
2 Shake the bitters over the ice.
3 Add the sugar and whisky.
4 Stir gently and serve.

Bothwell

you will need for 1 glass:

4–5 ice cubes
2–3 drops Angostura bitters
1 part Cointreau
3 parts whisky

1 Put the ice cubes into a glass jug.
2 Dash the bitters over the ice.
3 Add the Cointreau and whisky, stir vigorously, strain and pour into a chilled martini glass.

Whiz Bang

you will need for 1 glass:

4–5 ice cubes
3 drops orange bitters
½ teaspoon grenadine
1 part dry French vermouth
3 parts whisky
1 drop Pernod

1 Put the ice cubes into a glass jug.
2 Shake the orange bitters over the ice.
3 Pour in the grenadine, vermouth and whisky.
4 Stir vigorously, strain and pour into a chilled martini glass.
5 Put the Pernod in the mixture and serve.

Glasgow

you will need for 1 glass:

4–5 ice cubes
3 drops Angostura bitters
3 drops Pernod
1 part dry French vermouth
3 parts whisky

1 Put the ice cubes into a glass jug.
2 Shake the bitters and the Pernod over the ice.
3 Pour in the vermouth and whisky.
4 Stir vigorously, strain and pour into a chilled martini glass.

Borden

you will need for 1 glass:

4–5 ice cubes
2 drops Angostura bitters
3 drops Pernod
1 part sweet Italian vermouth
3 parts whisky

1 Put the ice cubes into a glass jug.
2 Shake the bitters and the Pernod over the ice.
3 Pour in the vermouth and whisky.
4 Stir vigorously, strain and pour into a chilled martini glass.

Jamie

you will need for 1 glass:

3–4 ice cubes
2 measures whisky
3 drops orange bitters or Angostura bitters
2 drops dry French vermouth
3 drops Cointreau

1 Put the ice cubes into a glass jug.
2 Pour the bitters, vermouth and Cointreau over the ice. Add the whisky.
3 Stir evenly, and pour without straining into a lowball glass.

Scots Guards

you will need for 1 glass:

4–5 ice cubes
juice 1 fresh lemon
juice ½ fresh orange
½ teaspoon grenadine
3 parts whisky

1 Put the ice cubes into a glass jug.
2 Pour the fruit juices, grenadine and whisky over the ice.
3 Stir vigorously, strain and pour into a chilled martini glass.

Benedict

you will need for 1 glass:

3–4 ice cubes
1 part Bénédictine
3 parts whisky
dry ginger ale

1 Put the ice cubes into a glass jug.
2 Pour the Bénédictine and whisky over the ice.
3 Stir evenly without splashing and, without straining, pour into a glass.
4 Top with dry ginger ale.

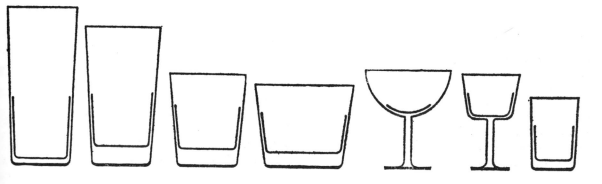

Bunny Hug

you will need for 1 glass:

4–5 ice cubes	1 part gin
1 part Pernod	3 parts whisky

1 Put the ice cubes into a glass jug.
2 Pour the Pernod, gin and whisky over the ice.
3 Stir vigorously, strain and pour into a chilled martini glass.

Chancellor

you will need for 1 glass:

4–5 ice cubes	1 part dry French
3 drops Angostura	vermouth
bitters	3 parts whisky
1 part port	1 slice fresh lemon rind

1 Put the ice cubes into a glass jug.
2 Shake the bitters over the ice.
3 Pour in the port, vermouth, and whisky over the ice.
4 Stir vigorously, strain and pour into a chilled martini glass.
5 Twist the fresh lemon rind over the mixture and drop it in.

Bill Orr

you will need for 1 glass:

4–5 ice cubes	juice ½ fresh orange (or
3 drops orange bitters	2 tablespoons canned,
or Angostura bitters	unsweetened)
	2 parts whisky

1 Put the ice cubes into a glass jug.
2 Dash bitters over the ice.
3 Pour in the orange juice and whisky.
4 Stir vigorously, strain and pour into a chilled martini glass.

American recipes

Most of the following recipes are typically American. Strictly speaking the principal ingredient should be either rye or bourbon or Canadian whisky. In most cases Scotch will do, but its flavour is smoother and subtler, and in fact it is too good a drink for such mixtures.

Brainstorm

you will need for 1 glass:

4–5 ice cubes	2 parts bourbon or
1 part dry French	Scotch whisky
vermouth	1 slice fresh orange rind
1 part Bénédictine	

1 Put the ice cubes into a glass jug.
2 Pour the vermouth, Bénédictine and bourbon over the ice.
3 Stir vigorously, strain and pour into a chilled martini glass.
4 Garnish with the orange rind and serve.

Chauncey

you will need for 1 glass:

4–5 ice cubes	1 part gin
3 drops Angostura	1 part brandy
bitters	2 parts bourbon or
1 part sweet Italian	Scotch whisky
vermouth	

1 Put the ice cubes into a glass jug.
2 Shake the bitters over the ice.
3 Pour in the vermouth, gin, brandy and bourbon.
4 Stir vigorously, strain and pour into a chilled martini glass.

Harrity

you will need for 1 glass:

4–5 ice cubes
3 drops Angostura
  bitters
1 part gin
3 parts bourbon or
  Scotch whisky

1 Put the ice cubes into a glass jug.
2 Shake the bitters over the ice.
3 Pour in the gin and whisky, stir vigorously, strain and pour into a chilled martini glass.

Hearns

you will need for 1 glass:

4–5 ice cubes
3 drops Angostura
  bitters
1 part Pernod
1 part dry French
  vermouth
2 parts bourbon or
  Scotch whisky

1 Put the ice cubes into a glass jug.
2 Shake the bitters over the ice.
3 Pour in the Pernod, vermouth and bourbon.
4 Stir vigorously, strain and pour into a chilled martini glass.

Liberal

you will need for 1 glass:

4–5 ice cubes
3 drops orange bitters
  or Angostura bitters
1 part sweet Italian
  vermouth
½ part Amer Picon
3 parts bourbon or
  Scotch whisky
1 slice fresh orange rind

1 Put the ice cubes into a glass jug.
2 Shake the bitters over the ice.
3 Pour in the vermouth, Amer Picon, and bourbon.
4 Stir vigorously, and pour without straining into a lowball glass.
5 Garnish with the orange rind and serve.

McCrory

you will need for 1 glass:

4–5 ice cubes
3 drops Angostura
  bitters
½ teaspoon sugar or
  sugar syrup
2 parts bourbon or
  Scotch whisky

1 Put the ice cubes into a glass jug.
2 Shake the bitters over the ice.
3 Pour the sugar and bourbon on to the ice.
4 Stir vigorously, and pour, without straining, into a lowball glass.

McKinley's Delight

you will need for 1 glass:

4–5 ice cubes
3 drops Pernod
½ teaspoon cherry
  brandy
1 part sweet Italian
  vermouth
2 parts bourbon or
  Scotch whisky

1 Put the ice cubes into a glass jug.
2 Shake the Pernod over the ice.
3 Add the cherry brandy and the vermouth and bourbon.
4 Stir vigorously, strain and pour into a chilled martini glass.

Whisky Royal

you will need for 1 glass:

4–5 ice cubes
3 drops orange bitters
  or Angostura bitters
3 parts rye or Scotch
  whisky
2 drops white crème de
  menthe

1 Put the ice cubes into a glass jug.
2 Shake the bitters over the ice.
3 Add the rye, stir vigorously, and pour, without straining, into a lowball glass.
4 Drop the crème de menthe on to the mixture and serve.

Suburban

you will need for 1 glass:

4–5 ice cubes
3 drops orange bitters
  or Angostura bitters
1 part port
1 part dark rum
3 parts bourbon or
  Scotch whisky

1 Put the ice cubes into a glass jug.
2 Shake the bitters over the ice.
3 Pour in the port, rum and bourbon.
4 Stir vigorously, strain and pour into a chilled martini glass.

Algonquin

you will need for 1 glass:

4–5 ice cubes
1 part unsweetened
  pineapple juice
1 part dry French
  vermouth
3 parts bourbon or
  Scotch whisky

1 Put the ice cubes into a glass jug.
2 Pour the pineapple juice, vermouth and bourbon over the ice.
3 Stir vigorously, until nearly frothy, strain and pour into a chilled martini glass.

Walter's

you will need for 1 glass:

4–5 ice cubes
juice ½ fresh lemon
juice ½ fresh orange
3 parts bourbon or
  Scotch whisky

1 Put the ice cubes into a glass jug.
2 Pour the fruit juices and whisky over the ice.
3 Stir vigorously, strain and pour into a chilled martini glass.

Cliquet

you will need for 1 glass:

4–5 ice cubes
juice 1 fresh orange (or
  4 tablespoons canned,
  unsweetened juice)
1 tablespoon dark rum
3 parts bourbon or
  Scotch whisky

1 Put the ice cubes into a glass jug.
2 Pour the orange juice, rum and bourbon over the ice.
3 Stir vigorously, strain and pour into a sour glass.

Woodward

you will need for 1 glass:

4–5 ice cubes
juice ½ fresh grapefruit
  (or 2½ tablespoons
  canned, unsweetened
  juice)
1 part dry French
  vermouth
3 parts bourbon or
  Scotch whisky

1 Put the ice cubes into a glass jug.
2 Pour the grapefruit juice, vermouth and whisky over the ice.
3 Stir vigorously, strain and pour into a chilled martini glass.

Skipper

you will need for 1 glass:

4–5 ice cubes
4 drops grenadine
juice ½ fresh orange (or
  2 tablespoons canned,
  unsweetened juice)
1 part dry French
  vermouth
3 parts rye or Scotch
  whisky

1 Put the ice cubes into a glass jug.
2 Pour the grenadine over the ice.
3 Add the orange juice, vermouth and rye.
4 Stir vigorously, until nearly frothy, strain and pour into a sour glass.

Thompson

you will need for 1 glass:

4–5 ice cubes
3 drops Angostura or orange bitters
1 part dry French vermouth
3 parts rye or Scotch whisky
1 slice fresh lemon rind
1 slice fresh orange rind
1 wedge canned or fresh pineapple

1 Put the ice cubes into a glass jug.
2 Shake the bitters over the ice.
3 Pour the vermouth and rye into the jug.
4 Stir evenly, and pour without straining into a lowball glass.
5 Twist the lemon rind over the mixture and drop it in.
6 Garnish with the orange rind and pineapple.

The Boy

you will need for 1 glass:

4–5 ice cubes
3 drops Angostura bitters
juice 1 fresh lemon
1 part Bénédictine
3 parts rye or Scotch whisky

1 Put the ice cubes into a glass jug.
2 Shake the bitters over the ice.
3 Pour in the lemon juice, Bénédictine and rye.
4 Stir vigorously, strain and pour into a sour glass.

Long drinks that are shaken

Whisky Collins or Tom Collins (John Collins in U.S.A.)

you will need for 1 glass:

5–6 ice cubes
juice 1 fresh lemon
1 tablespoon sugar or sugar syrup
3 parts whisky
1 slice fresh orange
1 maraschino cherry (optional)
soda water

1 Put the ice cubes into a cocktail shaker.
2 Pour the lemon juice, sugar and whisky over the ice.
3 Shake until a frost forms.
4 Pour without straining into a collins glass.
5 Garnish with the fruit.
6 Top with the soda, stir lightly and serve.

4 Drop in the hulls of the lime. Add the cherry and top with soda water.
5 Stir gently and serve.

Nerida

you will need for 1 glass:

4–5 ice cubes
juice ½ lime or lemon
3 parts whisky
dry ginger ale

1 Put the ice cubes into a cocktail shaker.
2 Pour the fruit juice and whisky over the ice.
3 Shake until a frost forms, and pour without straining into a collins glass.
4 Top with ginger ale, stir gently and serve.

Whiskey Rickey

you will need for 1 glass:

5–6 ice cubes
juice 1 fresh lime
3 parts whisky
1 maraschino cherry (optional)
soda water

1 Put the ice cubes into a cocktail shaker.
2 Pour the lime juice and whisky over the ice.
3 Shake until a frost forms; pour without straining into a collins glass.

Milk Punch

you will need for 1 glass:

4–5 ice cubes
1 teaspoon sugar or sugar syrup
2 parts whisky
3 parts milk
grated nutmeg

1 Put the ice cubes into a cocktail shaker.
2 Pour the sugar, whisky and milk over the ice.
3 Shake until a frost forms.
4 Pour without straining into a highball glass.
5 Sprinkle the top with nutmeg and serve.

Short drinks that are shaken

Scotch Sour
you will need for 1 glass:

4–5 ice cubes
2 drops Angostura
  bitters
juice 1 fresh lemon

1 teaspoon sugar or
  sugar syrup
3 parts whisky
1 maraschino cherry
  (optional)

1 Put the ice cubes into a cocktail shaker.
2 Shake the bitters over the ice.
3 Pour in the lemon juice, sugar and whisky.
4 Shake until a frost forms.
5 Strain and pour into a sour glass.
6 Garnish with the cherry and serve.

Tar
you will need for 1 glass:

4–5 ice cubes
juice 1 fresh lemon
¼ teaspoon grenadine

1 part crème de cacao
3 parts whisky

1 Put the ice cubes into a cocktail shaker.
2 Pour in the lemon juice, the grenadine, crème de cacao and whisky.
3 Shake until a frost forms, strain and pour into a glass.

Flordita
you will need for 1 glass:

4–5 ice cubes
3 drops Angostura
  bitters
¼ teaspoon sugar or
  sugar syrup

¼ part Amer Picon
1 part Curaçao
1 part sweet Italian
  vermouth
3 parts whisky

1 Put the ice cubes into a cocktail shaker.
2 Shake the bitters over the ice.
3 Pour in the sugar, Amer Picon, Curaçao, vermouth and whisky.
4 Shake until a frost forms, strain and pour into a lowball glass.

Clear Skies Ahead
you will need for 1 glass:

1 egg white
4–5 ice cubes
¼ teaspoon sugar

juice ¼ fresh lemon
¼ teaspoon grenadine
2 parts whisky

1 Put the ice cubes into a cocktail shaker.
2 Pour in the sugar, lemon juice, grenadine, egg white and whisky.
3 Shake until a frost forms, strain and pour into a sour glass.

Whisky Flip
you will need for 1 glass:

4–5 ice cubes
1 egg

½ teaspoon sugar or
  sugar syrup
2 parts whisky

1 Put the ice cubes into a cocktail shaker.
2 Pour the egg, sugar and whisky over the ice.
3 Shake until frost forms, strain and pour into a sherry glass.

Millionaire
you will need for 1 glass:

1 egg white
4–5 ice cubes
3 drops grenadine

1 part Curaçao
3 parts whisky

1 Put the ice cubes into a cocktail shaker.
2 Pour the grenadine, the Curaçao, and whisky over the ice.
3 Add the egg white and shake the mixture until a frost forms.
4 Strain and pour into a chilled martini glass.

Pretoria
you will need for 1 glass:

4–5 ice cubes
juice ½ fresh grapefruit
  (or 2½ tablespoons
  canned unsweetened
  juice)

1 part dry French
  vermouth
3 parts whisky
1 maraschino cherry

1 Put the ice cubes into a cocktail shaker.
2 Pour the grapefruit juice, vermouth and whisky over the ice.
3 Shake until a frost forms; strain and pour into a chilled martini glass.
4 Garnish with the cherry and serve.

Golden Daisy

you will need for 1 glass:

4-5 ice cubes
juice 1 fresh lemon
1 teaspoon sugar or
   sugar syrup
½ part Cointreau
3 parts whisky

1 Put the ice cubes into a cocktail shaker.
2 Pour the lemon juice, sugar, Cointreau and whisky over the ice.
3 Shake vigorously until a frost forms.
4 Strain and pour into a sour glass *or* pour without straining into a highball glass and serve with drinking straws.

Eliot

you will need for 1 glass:

4-5 ice cubes
juice 1 fresh lemon
1 teaspoon sugar or
   sugar syrup
2 parts port
3 parts whisky
1 egg white

1 Put the ice cubes into a cocktail shaker.
2 Pour the lemon juice, sugar, port, whisky and egg white over the ice.
3 Shake until a frost forms; strain and pour into a sour glass.

Drinks for a heatwave

Scotch Mist

you will need for 1 glass:

crushed ice
1 sprig tender mint
2 measures whisky

1 Fill an old-fashioned glass with crushed ice.
2 Stuff the mint leaves into the ice and swirl them about.
3 Pour in the whisky, stir gently and serve.

Mississippi Punch

you will need for 1 glass:

crushed ice
3 drops Angostura
   bitters
1 teaspoon sugar or
   sugar syrup
juice 1 fresh lemon
1 part brandy
1 part dark rum
2 parts whisky

1 Fill a collins glass with crushed ice.
2 Shake the bitters over the ice.
3 Pour in the sugar and lemon juice; stir gently to mix thoroughly.
4 Add the brandy, rum and whisky, *in that order*; stir once and serve with drinking straws.

Juleps

Purists agree that the perfect way of making a Julep is to use bourbon and to serve it in a silver mug. After that there are as many variants as you please. The preparations for Juleps are complicated and time consuming. Firstly the mug, or glass, must be thoroughly chilled, if not iced. Secondly only crushed ice, ice that has been pounded and dried as much as possible, should be used. Thirdly, in preparation the mug must not be touched. If a silver mug is not available, a collins glass can be used instead.

Louisville Mint Julep

you will need for 1 glass:

1 teaspoon sugar or sugar syrup
3 sprigs fresh young mint
crushed ice
3 parts bourbon or Scotch whisky

1 Put the sugar into the base of an iced mug or glass.
2 Add the mint and stir to mix it gently with the sugar.
3 Pack crushed ice into the glass.
4 Pour the whisky over the ice, stirring it gently.
5 Add more crushed ice, stir until frost forms.
6 Wrap the mug with a table napkin but do not touch the mug with bare fingers or the frost will disappear.

Virginia Mint Julep

you will need for 1 glass:

9 sprigs tender young mint
1 teaspoon sugar or sugar syrup
crushed ice
3 parts bourbon or Scotch whisky

1 Put 6 sprigs of young mint into an iced mug or glass.
2 Pour in the sugar, crush the mint into the sugar with a spoon or pestle.
3 Fill the mug or glass with dry crushed ice; pour the whisky over the ice and stir gently.
4 Pack in more crushed ice, stir until frost appears.
5 Fix three sprigs of mint into the top of the drink.
6 Wrap with a table napkin and serve.

Tennessee Mint Julep

you will need for 1 glass:

9 sprigs tender young mint
1 teaspoon sugar syrup*
crushed ice
3 parts bourbon or Scotch whisky

*do not substitute sugar

1 Put 6 sprigs of mint into the iced mug or glass.
2 Add half the sugar syrup, and with a mixing spoon crush the mint into the sugar syrup, spreading it along the sides.
3 Pack the mug or glass with dry crushed ice, add the remaining sugar syrup.
4 Pour the whisky over the ice, stir gently.
5 Add more crushed ice, stir until frost forms.
6 Fix three sprigs of mint into the top of the glass.
7 Wrap with a table napkin and serve.

DO IT PROPERLY
MIXING THE PERFECT MARGARITA

Celebrate the arrival of summer with the classic Mexican cocktail. Top bar manager **Blake Perrow** shares his secrets

The margarita is one of those classic cocktails that says without doubt the summer is here. A little like the Glorious Twelfth

■ **The tequila:** "A good-quality silver (or blanco) tequila will give a bright, rustic flavour. Depends on your taste, but I use a richer 'gold' or 'reposado' variety. Cuervo is fine. It's a waste to use 'Anejo' – the aged version – in a strongly flavoured margarita, and anyway the taste is too refined."

■ **The limes:** "Keep them a week or so to ensure they are really ripe, it sweetens them and they get juicier too."

■ **The sweetener:** "Cointreau is great if you like a sweeter drink, Triple Sec makes it a little drier. Or substitute a dash of Agave Nectar if you can find it in health shops: it's a natural sweetener and really makes a difference.

HOW TO EMAIL PROPERLY

■ We all know correct form in letter-writing, but emails bring with them a quagmire of potential social gaffes. How does one open and close an email, for instance? Being British we felt we needed rules of polite engagement. Fleur Britten, author of a *Debrett's Etiquette guide*, says:

Always be kend communiqués with pleasantries, or they can read with unintended abruptness. Most greetings may be meaningless platitudes, but bland is better than off-hand.

When selecting your tops and tails, consider your relationship and the recipient's age and profession (the media, predictably, is more kissy-kissy than academia). In all cases, apply a sliding scale of respect versus affection; creativity should be reserved for the intimate end of the scale. Follow your correspondent's lead if possible.

TOPS:

heralding the shooting season, we feel that from the Mexican holiday of Cinco de Mayo onwards, margaritas may be quaffed with abandon, preferably by the brace.

But what is the perfect margarita recipe?

Step forward Blake "I'm Mexican in spirit" Perrow, general manager of La Perla Mexican restaurant in Covent Garden, London (sister to the oldest Mexican in London, Café Pacifico) and a true tequila aficionado.

"Like most good cocktails, the recipe is very simple but easy to make badly," he says. "The art comes in using the proper ratio of ingredients to balance the flavours."

They are:
4cl tequila
3cl freshly squeezed lime juice
2cl Triple Sec or Cointreau

★★★ **YOU'VE GOT MAIL** Move over, boring barbecues. This outrageous Barbie-coloured barbie will wake up your terrace no end. And it opens to provide double the amount of grilling space you'd expect. The only problem is how to colour co-ordinate the kebabs. £29.95 from the Linda Barker catalogue, 0870 242 0651.

...really enhances the flavour of the tequila."

■ **The glass:** "Run a lime around the rim and dip upside down in a saucer of salt. Shake off excess – you don't want the salt in the drink."

METHOD
Use a small handful of ice per drink
■ **Frozen (blended) margarita:** "Blitz all the ingredients together for a few seconds if you like it slushy."
■ **On the rocks:** "Rattle everything together in a chilled shaker and pour it unstrained."
■ **Straight up:** "Chill the glass first. Shake all the ingredients together but strain into the cold glass, leaving the ice behind.
"Either way, squeeze a good wedge of lime into the finished article and drop it into the drink. Sip through the salt, NOT with a straw. And Salud!"

'Dear' is making a comeback – its relative scarcity makes the word 'dear' flattering again, and is failsafe for business and personal relations of any longevity.

More informally, 'Hello' carries more charm than 'Hi' – both are adequate for addressing all but those of super-status (use 'Dear' if in doubt). 'Hey' merely says ageing-politician-does-groovy. Following with 'Hope all's well' can soften any impending blow.

TAILS:
'Best wishes' and 'Warm (or kind) regards' may not be the most inventive of send-offs, but for first-time overtures they are safer than anything more casual. 'Yours sincerely' should be consigned to the written letter.

'Very best wishes' affords a little more impact, whereas 'Best' can sound dismissive and self-important. Drop a kiss only if you would social-kiss in person.
And if in doubt, err towards the polite. ■
Debrett's Etiquette for Girls by Fleur Britten, £17.99.

Rum Drinks

Rum comes in a range of colours and flavours; white, golden and dark (or black). Made basically of sugar cane by-products most of the world's supply is made in the West Indies.

Each island and group has its own type: Cuban rums are generally lighter textured than those of Jamaica, Barbados, or Haïti. Some of the French West Indian rums from Martinique and Guadaloupe are very sweet, while the clear white rum from Trinidad is nearly as sharp as vodka.

It is the amount of burnt sugar cane syrup, or caramel, that gives colour and flavour to the drink. Many of the native mixed drinks are made of a mixture of rums.

Long drinks that are stirred

Rum and Soda

you will need for 1 glass:

3–4 ice cubes
2 parts golden rum
3 parts soda water
1 slice fresh lemon

1 Put the ice cubes into a highball glass.
2 Pour in the rum and soda water.
3 Garnish with the slice of lemon; stir gently and serve.

Rum and Dry Ginger

you will need for 1 glass:

3–4 ice cubes
2 parts white or golden rum
3 parts dry ginger ale
1 slice fresh lemon

1 Put the ice cubes into a highball glass.
2 Pour in the rum and ginger ale.
3 Garnish with the slice of lemon; stir gently and serve.

Cooper Cooler

you will need for 1 glass:

3–4 ice cubes
2 parts golden rum
3 parts dry ginger ale
1 tablespoon fresh lime juice or lemon juice
1 slice lime or lemon

1 Pour the ice cubes into a highball glass.
2 Pour in the rum and dry ginger and fruit juice.
3 Garnish with the slice of fruit and serve.

Rum and Coke

you will need for 1 glass:

3–4 ice cubes
2 parts golden or dark rum
3 parts coca cola
1 slice fresh lemon (optional)

1 Put the ice cubes into a highball glass.
2 Pour in the rum and coca cola.
3 Garnish with the slice of fruit; stir gently and serve.

Cuba Libré

you will need for 1 glass:

3–4 ice cubes
2 parts golden or dark rum
3 parts coca cola
juice and hull $\frac{1}{2}$ fresh lime or fresh lemon

1 Put the ice cubes into a highball glass.
2 Pour in the rum, coca cola and fruit juice.
3 Stir gently; drop in the fruit and serve.

St. George's Club

you will need for 1 glass:

3–4 ice cubes
2 parts white or golden rum
3 parts tonic water
1 slice fresh lime or lemon

1 Put the ice cubes into a highball glass.
2 Pour in the rum and tonic water.
3 Garnish with the fresh fruit; stir and serve.

Julien

you will need for 1 glass:

3–4 ice cubes
3 drops Angostura bitters
juice 1 fresh lime or lemon
2 parts white or golden rum
3 parts tonic water
1 slice fresh lime or lemon

1 Put the ice cubes into a highball glass.
2 Shake the bitters on the ice.
3 Pour in the fruit juice, rum and tonic water.
4 Garnish with the fresh fruit; stir and serve.

St. James

you will need for 1 glass:

3–4 ice cubes
Juice ½ fresh lime or lemon
Juice 1 fresh orange (or 4 tablespoons canned, unsweetened)
3 drops Angostura bitters
2 parts white or golden rum
2 parts tonic water
1 slice fresh lime or lemon

1 Put the ice cubes into a highball glass.
2 Pour in the fruit juice.
3 Shake the bitters on the ice.
4 Add the rum and tonic water.
5 Garnish with fresh fruit; stir gently and serve.

Point Saline

you will need for 1 glass:

3–4 ice cubes
juice ½ fresh lime or lemon
juice 1 fresh orange (or 4 tablespoons canned, unsweetened juice)
2 drops Angostura bitters
1 teaspoon sugar or sugar syrup
2 parts white or golden rum
3 parts soda water
1 slice fresh lime or lemon
sprig fresh mint (optional)

1 Put the ice cubes into a highball glass.
2 Pour in the fruit juices.
3 Shake the bitters over the ice.
4 Add the sugar and rum; stir gently.
5 Add the soda.
6 Garnish with fresh fruit and serve.

Rum Rickey

you will need for 1 glass:

3–4 ice cubes
juice 1 fresh lime
2 parts white or golden rum
3 parts soda water
flesh ½ lime
1 maraschino cherry (optional)

1 Put the ice cubes into a collins glass.
2 Pour in the lime juice, rum and soda water.
3 Drop in the flesh of the lime; stir gently.
4 Garnish with the cherry and serve.

Piña

you will need for 1 glass:

3–4 ice cubes
Angostura bitters
1 part pineapple juice
2 parts white or golden rum
3 parts soda water

1 Put the ice cubes into a collins glass.
2 Pour in the bitters, pineapple juice and rum.
3 Stir thoroughly.
4 Pour in the soda water; stir gently, and serve.

Rum and Orange

you will need for 1 glass:

3–4 ice cubes
juice 1 fresh orange
2 parts white or golden rum
3 parts soda water or water

1 Put the ice cubes into a highball glass.
2 Pour in the orange juice and rum.
3 Stir to mix thoroughly.
4 Add the soda water and serve.

Rum and Lime

you will need for 1 glass:

3–4 ice cubes
1 part bottle lime juice
2 parts white or golden rum
3 parts water
1 sprig fresh mint (optional)

1 Put the ice cubes into a highball glass.
2 Pour in the lime juice and rum.
3 Stir to mix thoroughly.
4 Add the water and fresh mint.
5 Stir gently and serve.

Short drinks that are stirred

Rum Old-Fashioned

you will need for 1 glass:

1 cube sugar
2 drops Angostura
  bitters
2–3 ice cubes

2 parts golden or dark
  rum
1 slice fresh lemon or
  orange (optional)

1 Put the cube of sugar in the base of an old-fashioned glass.
2 Shake the bitters on to the sugar. Swirl this around the glass. Add ice cubes.
3 Pour in the rum; stir gently.
4 Garnish with fruit and serve.

Pink Rum

you will need for 1 glass:

3 drops Angostura
  bitters
2 parts white or golden
  rum

3 parts ice cold water

1 Shake the bitters into a sour glass and swirl them around.
2 Pour in the rum and ice cold water.

Rum Martini

you will need for 1 glass:

4–5 ice cubes
1 part dry French
  vermouth

3 parts white rum
1 slice fresh lemon rind

1 Put the ice cubes into a glass jug.
2 Pour the vermouth and rum over the ice.
3 Stir vigorously; strain and pour into a chilled martini glass.
4 Twist the fresh lemon rind over the drink and drop it in.

Rum Perfect

you will need for 1 glass:

4–5 ice cubes
½ part dry French
  vermouth
½ part sweet Italian
  vermouth

3 parts white or golden
  rum
1 slice fresh lemon rind

1 Put the ice cubes into a glass jug.
2 Pour the vermouths and rum over the ice.
3 Stir vigorously, strain and pour into a chilled martini glass.
4 Twist the lemon rind over the drink and drop it in.

Rum Manhattan

you will need for 1 glass:

4–5 ice cubes
1 part sweet Italian
  vermouth

3 parts white or golden
  rum
1 maraschino cherry

1 Put the ice cubes into a glass jug.
2 Pour the vermouth and rum over the ice.
3 Stir vigorously; strain and pour into a chilled martini glass.
4 Drop in the cherry and serve.

Rum Gimlet

you will need for 1 glass:

3–4 ice cubes
1 part bottle lime juice

3 parts white or golden
  rum

1 Put the ice cubes into a glass jug.
2 Pour in the lime juice and rum.
3 Stir vigorously; strain and pour into a chilled martini glass.

Bridgetown

you will need for 1 glass:

4–5 ice cubes
1 part pineapple juice
1 part dry French
  vermouth
3 parts white rum
½ teaspoon grenadine

1 Put the ice cubes into a glass jug.
2 Pour the pineapple juice, vermouth, rum and grenadine over the ice.
3 Stir vigorously; strain and pour into a chilled martini glass.

Port Antonio

you will need for 1 glass:

4–5 ice cubes
1 part fresh lime juice
3 parts white or golden
  rum
½ teaspoon grenadine
1 slice fresh lime rind

1 Put the ice cubes into a glass jug.
2 Pour the lime juice, rum and grenadine over the ice.
3 Stir vigorously; strain and pour into a chilled martini glass.
4 Twist the lime rind over the drink and drop it in.

Port-au-Prince

you will need for 1 glass:

1 lump sugar
3 drops Peychaud
  bitters or Angostura
  bitters
3 parts dark rum
3–4 drops Pernod
3–4 ice cubes
1 slice fresh lime rind or
  lemon rind

1 Put the cube of sugar in the base of a glass.
2 Shake the bitters on to the rum, add the Pernod.
3 Swirl the mixture around the glass, crushing the sugar.
4 Put the ice cubes into the glass.
5 Pour the rum over the ice cubes.
6 Stir gently; squeeze the lime rind over the mixture and serve.

Rum Sidecar

you will need for 1 glass:

4–5 ice cubes
juice 1 fresh lemon
1 part Triple Sec
3 parts white or golden
  rum

1 Put the ice cubes into a glass jug.
2 Pour the lemon juice, Triple Sec and rum over the ice.
3 Stir vigorously; strain and pour into a chilled martini glass.

Rum Dubonnet

you will need for 1 glass:

4–5 ice cubes
1 part Dubonnet
3 parts white rum
1 slice fresh lime rind
  or lemon rind

1 Put the ice cubes into a glass jug.
2 Pour the Dubonnet and rum over the ice.
3 Stir vigorously; strain and pour into a chilled martini glass.
4 Twist the lime rind over the mixture and drop it in.

Grenada Cocktail

you will need for 1 glass:

4–5 ice cubes
juice ½ fresh orange (or
  2 tablespoons canned,
  unsweetened juice)
1 part sweet Italian
  vermouth
3 parts golden or dark
  rum
powdered cinnamon

1 Put the ice cubes into a glass jug.
2 Pour the orange juice, vermouth and rum over the ice.
3 Stir vigorously; strain and pour into a chilled martini glass.
4 Sprinkle a bit of cinnamon on top and serve.

Batiste

you will need for 1 glass:

4–5 ice cubes
1 part Grand Marnier

2 parts golden or dark
rum

1 Put the ice cubes into a glass jug.
2 Pour the Grand Marnier and rum over the ice.
3 Stir vigorously; strain and pour into a martini glass.

Chinese

you will need for 1 glass:

4–5 ice cubes
3 drops Angostura
bitters
½ teaspoon sugar or
sugar syrup

½ teaspoon grenadine
1 part Curaçao
3 parts golden or dark
rum

1 Put the ice cubes into a glass jug.
2 Shake the bitters over the ice.

3 Pour in the sugar, grenadine, Curaçao and rum.
4 Stir vigorously; strain and pour into a chilled martini glass.

Queen's Park

you will need for 1 glass:

4–5 ice cubes
juice 1 fresh lime or
lemon

1 teaspoon sugar or
sugar syrup
1 part whisky
2 parts dark rum

1 Put the ice cubes into a glass jug.
2 Pour the fruit juice, sugar, whisky and rum over the ice.
3 Stir vigorously; strain and pour into a chilled martini glass.

Long drinks that are shaken

Rum Collins

you will need for 1 glass:

4–5 ice cubes
juice 1 fresh lemon
1 teaspoon sugar or
sugar syrup

3 parts white or golden
rum
soda water
1 slice fresh lemon
1 sprig fresh mint

1 Put the ice cubes into a cocktail shaker.
2 Pour the lemon juice, sugar and rum over the ice.
3 Shake until frost forms.
4 Pour without straining into a collins glass.
5 Top with soda water and garnish with fruit and mint and serve.

Rico Chico

you will need for 1 glass:

4–5 ice cubes
1 teaspoon sugar or
sugar syrup
1 part gin

2 parts dark rum
dry ginger ale
1 slice fresh lime rind
or lemon rind

1 Put the ice cubes into a cocktail shaker.
2 Pour the sugar, gin and rum over the ice.
3 Shake until frost forms and pour without straining into a collins glass.
4 Top with ginger ale.
5 Garnish with fruit and serve.

Roaring River

you will need for 1 glass:

4–5 ice cubes
3 drops Angostura
bitters
¼ teaspoon grenadine
1 part gin

2 parts rum
1 teaspoon sugar or
sugar syrup
soda water

1 Put the ice cubes into a cocktail shaker.
2 Shake the bitters over the ice.
3 Pour in the grenadine, gin, rum and sugar.
4 Shake until a frost forms, and pour, without straining into a collins glass.
5 Top with soda water and serve.

Maracas Bay

you will need for 1 glass:

4–5 ice cubes
3 drops Angostura
bitters
juice 1 fresh lime or
lemon

1 teaspoon sugar or
sugar syrup
3 parts white rum
1 egg white
soda water

1 Whisk the egg white until stiff.
2 Put the ice cubes into a cocktail shaker.
3 Shake the bitters over the ice.
4 Pour in the fruit juice, sugar, rum and egg white.
5 Shake until a frost forms; pour without straining into a highball glass.
6 Top with soda water and serve.

Tobago Fizz

you will need for 1 glass:

4–5 ice cubes
juice ½ fresh lime or lemon
juice ¼ fresh orange (or 2 tablespoons canned, unsweetened juice)
3 parts golden rum
1 part thin cream
½ teaspoon sugar or sugar syrup
soda water (optional)

1 Put the ice cubes into a cocktail shaker.
2 Pour the fruit juices, rum, cream and sugar over the ice.
3 Shake until a frost forms; strain and pour into a glass *or* pour without straining into a highball glass.
4 Top with soda water and serve.

St. Lucia

you will need for 1 glass:

4–5 ice cubes
1 part Curaçao
1 part dry French vermouth
juice ¼ fresh orange (or 2 tablespoons canned, unsweetened juice)
1 teaspoon grenadine
2 parts white or golden rum

1 Put the ice cubes into a cocktail shaker.
2 Pour the Curaçao, vermouth, orange juice, grenadine and rum over the ice.
3 Shake until a frost forms and pour without straining into a highball glass.

Short drinks that are shaken

Rum Sour

you will need for 1 glass:

4–5 ice cubes
juice 1 fresh lime or lemon
1 teaspoon sugar or sugar syrup
3 parts golden or dark rum

1 Put the ice cubes into a cocktail shaker.
2 Pour the fruit juice, sugar and rum over the ice.
3 Shake until a frost forms; strain and pour into a sour glass.

Discovery Bay

you will need for 1 glass:

4–5 ice cubes
3 drops Angostura bitters
juice ½ fresh lime
1 teaspoon Curaçao
1 teaspoon sugar or sugar syrup
3 parts golden or dark rum

1 Put the ice cubes into a cocktail shaker.
2 Shake the bitters over the ice.

3 Pour in the lime juice, Curaçao, sugar and rum.
4 Shake until a frost forms.
5 Strain and pour into a sour glass.

Montego Bay

you will need for 1 glass:

4–5 ice cubes
juice ½ fresh lime or lemon
1 part white crème de menthe
3 parts white or golden rum
1 sprig fresh mint (optional)

1 Put the ice cubes into a cocktail shaker.
2 Pour the fruit juice, crème de menthe and rum over the ice.
3 Shake until a frost forms.
4 Strain and pour into a sour glass.
5 Garnish with mint and serve.

Rodney

you will need for 1 glass:

4–5 ice cubes
juice ½ fresh lime or
  lemon
juice ½ fresh orange (or
  2 tablespoons canned,
  unsweetened juice)

3 drops Angostura
  bitters
1 teaspoon sugar or
  sugar syrup
3–4 drops grenadine
3 parts white or golden
  rum

1 Put the ice cubes into a cocktail shaker.
2 Pour the fruit juices and bitters over the ice.
3 Add the sugar, grenadine and rum.
4 Shake until a frost forms.
5 Strain and pour into a sour glass.

Rum Curaçao

you will need for 1 glass:

4–5 ice cubes
3 drops Angostura
  bitters

1 part Curaçao
3 parts rum
1 slice fresh orange rind

1 Put the ice cubes into a cocktail shaker.
2 Shake the bitters over the ice.
3 Pour in the Curaçao and rum.
4 Shake until a frost forms.
5 Strain and pour into a sour glass and garnish with orange rind.

Christophe

you will need for 1 glass:

4–5 ice cubes
juice ½ fresh lime or
  lemon
1 teaspoon sugar or
  sugar syrup

1 part Bénédictine
2 parts golden or dark
  rum

1 Put the cubes into a cocktail shaker.
2 Pour the fruit juice, sugar, Bénédictine and rum over the ice.
3 Shake until a frost forms.
4 Strain and pour into a sour glass.

Petionville

you will need for 1 glass:

4–5 ice cubes
juice ½ fresh lime or
  lemon
juice ½ fresh orange (or
  2 tablespoons canned,
  unsweetened juice)
1 part Cointreau

3 parts golden or dark
  rum
1 slice fresh lime or
  lemon
1 slice orange
1 maraschino cherry
  (optional)

1 Put the ice cubes into a cocktail shaker.
2 Pour the fruit juices, Cointreau and rum over the ice.
3 Shake until a frost forms.
4 Strain and pour into a sour glass.
5 Garnish with fruit and serve.

Piña Fria

you will need for 1 glass:

4–5 ice cubes
1 part pineapple juice

3 drops Angostura
  bitters
2 parts white rum

1 Put the ice cubes into a cocktail shaker.
2 Pour in the pineapple juice, the bitters and the rum.
3 Shake thoroughly, until a heavy frost forms.
4 Strain and pour into a sour glass.

Bacardi Rum Cocktails

Bacardi cocktail is another of those mixed drinks about which there is a *mystique*. Like the dry martini cocktail there are many variations but to the experts prime requisites are essential—Bacardi rum, fresh fruit, lots and lots of ice and a great deal of shaking.

The Bacardi

you will need for 1 glass:

4–5 ice cubes
juice 1 fresh lime

1 teaspoon sugar or
  sugar syrup
3 parts Bacardi rum

1 Put the ice cubes into a cocktail shaker.
2 Pour the lime juice, sugar and rum over the ice.
3 Shake until a frost forms, strain and pour into a chilled martini glass.

Pink Bacardi

you will need for 1 glass:

4–5 ice cubes
juice 1 fresh lime
1 teaspoon sugar or
  sugar syrup

4–5 drops grenadine
3 parts light golden rum

1 Put the ice cubes into a cocktail shaker.
2 Pour the lime juice, sugar, grenadine and rum over the ice.
3 Shake until a frost forms.
4 Strain and pour into a chilled martini glass.

Pale Pink Bacardi

you will need for 1 glass:

4–5 ice cubes
juice 1 fresh lime
1 teaspoon sugar or
  sugar syrup

4–5 drops grenadine
2 parts light golden rum
1 part gin

1 Put the ice cubes into a cocktail shaker.
2 Pour the lime juice, sugar, grenadine, rum and gin over the ice.
3 Shake until a frost forms; strain and pour into a chilled martini glass.

Daiquiri

you will need for 1 glass:

cracked ice
juice 2 fresh limes

1 teaspoon sugar or
  sugar syrup
3 parts white rum

1 Put lots of cracked ice into a cocktail shaker.
2 Pour the lime juice, sugar and rum over the ice.
3 Shake really thoroughly until a frost forms.
4 Pour and strain into an iced martini glass.

Frozen Daiquiri

you will need for 1 glass:

ice
juice 2 fresh limes

1 teaspoon sugar or
  sugar syrup
3 parts white rum

1 Put five or six ice cubes into a cocktail shaker.
2 Pour the lime juice, sugar and rum over the ice.
3 Pack a champagne glass full with finely *crushed* ice.
4 Shake the mixture until frost forms.
5 Strain and pour into the ice-packed champagne glass.
6 Serve with a short drinking straw.

Zombies

Like Juleps the recipes vary with the region of origin. In fact they vary from town to town as well as from island to island. The essentials are two or three types of rum, fresh fruit and lots of ice.

Havana Zombie

you will need for 1 glass:

4–5 ice cubes
juice fresh lime or
  lemon*
juice fresh pineapple
1 teaspoon sugar or
  sugar syrup

1 part white rum
1 part golden rum
1 part dark rum

*If fresh lemon juice is used instead of lime juice, use fresh orange juice in place of fresh pineapple juice.

1 Put the ice cubes into a glass jug.
2 Pour the fruit juices, sugar and rums over the ice.
3 Stir vigorously, and pour without straining into a collins glass.

Port-au-Prince Zombie

you will need for 1 glass:

4–5 ice cubes
juice 1 fresh lemon
juice 1 fresh orange
juice ½ fresh grapefruit
3 drops Angostura
  bitters

1 teaspoon soft brown
  sugar
1 part white rum
1 part golden rum
1 part dark rum

1 Put the ice cubes into a glass jug.
2 Pour the fruit juices over the ice and shake the bitters into the jug.
3 Add the brown sugar, and rums.
4 Stir vigorously, and pour without straining, into a collins glass.

Zombie Voodoo

you will need for 1 glass:

4–5 ice cubes
juice 1 fresh lime or lemon
juice ½ fresh orange (or 2 tablespoons canned, unsweetened juice)
3 drops Angostura bitters
1 teaspoon sugar or sugar syrup
1 egg white
1 part white rum
1 part golden rum
½ part dark rum
1 slice fresh orange
1 sprig fresh mint
1 maraschino cherry

1 Put the ice cubes into a cocktail shaker.
2 Pour the fruit juices over the ice and shake the bitters into the shaker.
3 Add the sugar, egg white, white and golden rum.
4 Shake until a frost forms.
5 Pour without straining into a collins glass.
6 Garnish with the fruit.
7 Top off with the dark rum.
8 Stir once and serve.

Zombie Christophe

you will need for 1 glass:

4–5 ice cubes
juice 1 fresh lime or lemon
juice ½ fresh orange
juice 1 fresh pineapple (or 1 8-oz. can unsweetened juice)
1 part Curaçao
1 part white rum
1 part golden rum
flesh ½ fresh lime or lemon
1 sprig mint
½ part dark rum

1 Put the ice cubes into a glass jug.
2 Pour the fruit juices, Curaçao, white and golden rums over the ice.
3 Stir vigorously, and pour without straining into a collins glass.
4 Garnish with the flesh of the fruit and mint.
5 Top with the dark rum.
6 Stir gently and serve.

Punches

No matter what the variation wherever Rum Punches are made in the Caribbean they are invariably delicious. Undoubtedly this standard of magnificence is maintained only by grace of the ever present profusion of fresh fruits. The best way to make your own punches is therefore to use only fresh fruit *and* sugar syrup. These drinks also improve by being kept in the refrigerator a few hours before serving.

Simple Punch

you will need for 1 glass:

juice 1 fresh lime
1 teaspoon sugar syrup
3 drops Angostura bitters
3 parts golden or dark rum
1 slice fresh orange
1 slice fresh lime
1 slice fresh lemon
1 wedge fresh pineapple
cracked ice
ground nutmeg

1 Put the lime juice and sugar syrup into a glass jug.
2 Shake the bitters into the mixture.
3 Add the rum and stir thoroughly.
4 Add the fresh fruit.
5 Store the mixture in a refrigerator for 3 hours.
6 Fill a lowball glass with cracked ice and, without straining, pour in the punch including the fruit.
7 Sprinkle the top with a little ground nutmeg and serve.

Barbados Punch

you will need for 1 glass:

juice 1 fresh lemon
juice 1 fresh orange
1 teaspoon sugar syrup
3 drops Angostura
  bitters

3 parts dark rum
1 slice fresh orange
1 wedge pineapple
cracked ice
ground nutmeg

1 Put the fruit juices and sugar syrup into a glass jug.
2 Shake the bitters into the mixture and add the rum and slices of fresh fruit.
3 Stir thoroughly and store it in the refrigerator for 3 hours.
4 Fill a lowball glass with cracked ice and pour in the punch without straining.
5 Sprinkle the top with nutmeg and serve.

Bahamas Punch

you will need for 1 glass:

juice 1 fresh lemon
1 teaspoon sugar syrup
3 drops Angostura
  bitters
½ teaspoon grenadine

3 parts golden or white
  rum
1 slice fresh orange
1 slice fresh lemon
cracked ice
ground nutmeg

1 Pour the lemon juice and syrup into a glass jug.
2 Shake the bitters into the mixture.
3 Add the grenadine, rum and slices of fresh fruit.
4 Stir thoroughly and store in the refrigerator for 3 hours.
5 Fill a lowball glass with cracked ice.
6 Pour in the unstrained punch.
7 Sprinkle the top with nutmeg and serve.

Punch Martiniquais

you will need for 1 glass:

juice 2 fresh limes
3 drops orange bitters
  or Angostura bitters
½ teaspoon grenadine
1 part Cointreau

3 parts dark rum
1 slice fresh lime
1 slice fresh orange
cracked ice
ground nutmeg

1 Put the lime juice into a glass jug and shake the bitters into it.
2 Add the grenadine, Cointreau, rum and fruit.

3 Stir thoroughly and store in a refrigerator for 3 hours.
4 Fill a lowball glass with cracked ice, and pour in the unstrained punch.
5 Sprinkle the top with nutmeg and serve.

Rum Wilhelmstädt

you will need for 1 glass:

juice 1 fresh lime
1 teaspoon sugar syrup
3 drops orange bitters
  or Angostura bitters
1 part crème de cacao
3 parts golden rum

1 slice fresh lime
1 slice fresh lemon
1 slice orange
cracked ice
1 extra tablespoon
  crème de cacao

1 Put the lime juice and sugar into a glass jug.
2 Shake the bitters into the mixture.
3 Pour in the crème de cacao, rum and add the fresh fruit.
4 Stir thoroughly and store it in the refrigerator for 3 hours.
5 Fill a lowball glass with cracked ice and pour in the unstrained punch.
6 Top with the extra crème de cacao.
7 Stir and serve.

Tobago Punch

you will need for 1 glass:

juice 1 fresh lime
juice 1 fresh orange
1 teaspoon sugar syrup
3 drops Angostura
  bitters
½ teaspoon grenadine
3 parts golden rum
1 slice fresh orange

1 slice fresh lime
1 slice fresh lemon
1 slice fresh pineapple
cracked ice
ground nutmeg
1 sprig fresh mint
  (optional)

1 Pour the fruit juices and syrup into a glass jug.
2 Shake the bitters over the mixture.
3 Add the grenadine, rum and fruits.
4 Stir thoroughly and store the mixture in the refrigerator for 3 hours.
5 Fill a lowball glass with cracked ice and pour the punch, including fruit, into it.
6 Sprinkle the top with nutmeg.
7 Garnish with mint and serve.

The Grenada Punch

you will need for 1 glass:

juice 1 fresh lime	3 parts dark rum
juice 1 fresh lemon	1 slice fresh lime
juice 1 fresh orange	1 slice fresh orange
1 teaspoon sugar syrup	1 slice fresh lemon
3 drops Angostura bitters	1 slice pineapple cracked ice
½ teaspoon grenadine	ground nutmeg

1 Pour the fruit juices and sugar into a glass jug.
2 Shake the bitters into the mixture.
3 Add the grenadine, rum and fresh fruit.
4 Stir thoroughly and store the mixture in the refrigerator for 3 hours.
5 Fill a lowball glass with cracked ice.
6 Pour the punch and the fruit over the ice.
7 Sprinkle the top with nutmeg and serve.

Punch Julien

you will need for 1 glass:

juice 2 fresh limes	3 parts dark rum
1 part pineapple juice (or canned, unsweetened)	1 slice fresh lime
	1 slice lemon
	1 slice orange
3 drops Angostura bitters	1 wedge pineapple cracked ice
½ teaspoon grenadine	ground nutmeg
1 part golden rum	

1 Pour the fruit juices and the bitters into a glass jug.
2 Add the grenadine, rums and fresh fruits.
3 Stir thoroughly and store for 3 hours in a refrigerator.
4 Fill a lowball glass with cracked ice.
5 Pour the punch and the fruit over the ice.
6 Sprinkle the top with nutmeg and serve.

Brandy Drinks

The word brandy comes from the original Dutch *brandtweijn* meaning burnt wine. It is a distillation of wine, as gin and whisky and vodka and rum are distillations of grain. It is best to use the younger brandies for mixed drinks. Older brandies, mellower and more expensive are too good for mixing and are quite spoiled. Save those, slightly warmed, for after dinner.

Brandy and Water
you will need for 1 glass:

2–3 ice cubes   water
1 measure brandy

1 Put the ice cubes into a highball glass.
2 Pour the brandy over the ice.
3 Add water to taste.

Brandy and Soda
you will need for 1 glass:

2–3 ice cubes   soda water
1 measure brandy

1 Put the ice cubes into a highball glass.
2 Pour the brandy over the ice.
3 Add soda water to taste.

Brandy and Ginger Ale
you will need for 1 glass:

2–3 ice cubes   ginger ale.
1 measure brandy

1 Put the ice cubes into a highball glass.
2 Pour the brandy over the ice.
3 Add ginger ale to taste.

Drinks that are stirred

Brandy Old-Fashioned
you will need for 1 glass:

1 cube sugar   1 part brandy
2 drops Angostura   1 slice lemon rind
  bitters   1 maraschino cherry
2–3 ice cubes   (optional)

1 Put the cube of sugar in the base of an old-fashioned glass.
2 Shake the bitters on to the sugar.
3 Swirl this about until it spreads to the sides.
4 Put the ice cubes into the glass and pour the brandy over them.
5 Stir gently.
6 Twist the lemon rind over the drink.
7 Garnish with the cherry and serve.

Brandy Sazerac
you will need for 1 glass:

1 cube sugar   5 drops Pernod
2 drops Peychaud   3 ice cubes
  bitters or Angostura   2 parts brandy
  bitters

1 Put the cube of sugar into the base of an old-fashioned glass.
2 Shake the bitters on to the sugar.
3 Add the Pernod.
4 Swirl this mixture around the glass.
5 Put the ice cubes into the glass and pour the brandy over them.
6 Stir gently and serve.

Brandy Toddler
you will need for 1 glass:

2–3 ice cubes   2 parts brandy
¼ teaspoon sugar or   water
  sugar syrup   1 slice fresh lemon rind

1 Put the ice cubes into an old-fashioned glass.
2 Pour the sugar and brandy over the ice.
3 Add a little water.
4 Twist the lemon rind over the mixture and drop it in.
5 Stir gently and serve.

Brandy Manhattan

you will need for 1 glass:

4–5 ice cubes
1 part sweet Italian vermouth
3 parts brandy
1 maraschino cherry (optional)

1 Put the ice cubes into a glass jug.
2 Pour the vermouth and brandy over the ice.
3 Stir vigorously; strain and pour into a chilled martini glass.
4 Garnish with the cherry.

Brandy Perfect

you will need for 1 glass:

4–5 ice cubes
½ part dry French vermouth
½ part sweet Italian vermouth
3 parts brandy
1 slice fresh lemon rind

1 Put the ice cubes into a glass jug.
2 Pour the vermouths and brandy over the ice.
3 Stir vigorously; strain and pour into a chilled martini glass.
4 Twist the lemon rind over the mixture and drop it in.

Paris

you will need for 1 glass:

4–5 ice cubes
5 drops Pernod
1 part dry French vermouth
3 parts brandy

1 Put the ice cubes into a glass jug.
2 Pour the Pernod, the vermouth and the brandy over the ice.
3 Stir vigorously; strain and pour into a chilled martini glass.

Balmoral

you will need for 1 glass:

4–5 ice cubes
3 drops Angostura bitters
1 part dry French vermouth
3 parts brandy

1 Put the ice cubes into a glass jug.
2 Shake the bitters and pour the vermouth and brandy over the ice.
3 Stir vigorously; strain and pour into a chilled martini glass.

Melbourne

you will need for 1 glass:

4–5 ice cubes
1 part Curaçao
3 parts brandy
1 slice fresh lemon rind

1 Put the ice cubes into a glass jug.
2 Pour the Curaçao and brandy over the ice.
3 Stir vigorously; strain and pour into a chilled martini glass.
4 Twist the lemon rind over the mixture and drop it in.

Mary Stuart

you will need for 1 glass:

4–5 ice cubes
1 part Drambuie
3 parts brandy
1 slice fresh lemon rind

1 Put the ice cubes into a glass jug.
2 Pour the Drambuie and brandy over the ice.
3 Stir vigorously; strain and pour into a chilled martini glass.
4 Twist the lemon rind over the mixture and drop it in.

MacDonald

you will need for 1 glass:

4–5 ice cubes
3 drops Angostura bitters
1 part Cointreau
3 parts brandy

1 Put the ice cubes into a glass jug.
2 Shake the bitters over the ice.
3 Add the Cointreau and brandy.
4 Stir vigorously; strain and pour into a chilled martini glass.

Friar

you will need for 1 glass:

4–5 ice cubes   3 parts brandy
1 part Bénédictine   water

1 Put the ice cubes into a glass jug.
2 Pour the Bénédictine and brandy over the ice.
3 Stir vigorously; strain and pour into a chilled martini glass.
4 Top with a little water and serve.

Fioupe

you will need for 1 glass:

4–5 ice cubes   1 part Bénédictine
1 part dry French   3 parts brandy
   vermouth   1 slice fresh lemon rind

1 Put the ice cubes into a glass jug.
2 Pour the vermouth, Bénédictine and brandy over the ice.
3 Stir vigorously; strain and pour into a chilled martini glass.
4 Twist the lemon rind over the mixture and drop it in.

Tours

you will need for 1 glass:

4–5 ice cubes   1 part dry French
3 drops Angostura   vermouth
   bitters   3 parts brandy
5 drops Pernod

1 Put the ice cubes into a glass jug.
2 Shake the bitters over the ice and add the Pernod.
3 Pour in the vermouth and brandy.
4 Stir vigorously; strain and pour into a chilled martini glass.

Darnley

you will need for 1 glass:

4–5 ice cubes   ½ teaspoon dry French
3 drops orange bitters   vermouth
   or Angostura bitters   1 part Cointreau
                    3 parts brandy

1 Put the ice cubes into a glass jug.
2 Shake the bitters over the ice and add the vermouth.
3 Pour in the Cointreau and brandy.
4 Stir vigorously; strain and pour into a chilled martini glass.

Nick's

you will need for 1 glass:

4–5 ice cubes   1 part sweet Italian
3 drops orange bitters   vermouth
   or Angostura bitters   3 parts brandy
5 drops Pernod

1 Put the ice cubes into a glass jug.
2 Shake the bitters over the ice and add the Pernod.
3 Pour in the vermouth and brandy.
4 Stir vigorously; strain and pour into a chilled martini glass.

Morning

you will need for 1 glass:

4–5 ice cubes   ½ teaspoon dry French
3 drops orange bitters   vermouth
   or Angostura bitters   1 part Curaçao
5 drops Pernod   3 parts brandy
½ teaspoon maraschino
   or grenadine

1 Put the ice cubes into a glass jug.
2 Shake the bitters over the ice, and add the Pernod.
3 Put in the grenadine, vermouth, Curaçao and brandy.
4 Stir vigorously; strain and pour into a chilled martini glass.

Whip

you will need for 1 glass:

4–5 ice cubes	1 part Curaçao
5 drops Pernod	2 parts brandy
1 part dry French vermouth	

1 Put the ice cubes into a glass jug.
2 Pour the Pernod, the vermouth, Curaçao and brandy over the ice.
3 Stir vigorously; strain and pour into a chilled martini glass.

Lord Chamberlain

you will need for 1 glass:

4–5 ice cubes	3 drops Angostura bitters
1 part port	
1 part dry French vermouth	2 parts brandy
	1 slice fresh lemon rind

1 Put the ice cubes into a glass jug.
2 Pour the port and vermouth over the ice.
3 Shake the bitters over the mixture and add the brandy.
4 Stir vigorously; strain and pour into a chilled martini glass.
5 Twist the lemon rind over the mixture and drop it in.

Independent

you will need for 1 glass:

4–5 ice cubes	½ part Amer Picon
3 drops orange bitters or Angostura bitters	3 parts brandy
	1 slice fresh orange rind
1 part sweet Italian vermouth	

1 Put the ice cubes into a glass jug.
2 Shake the bitters over the ice and add the vermouth, Amer Picon and brandy.
3 Stir vigorously; strain and pour into a chilled martini glass. Decorate with orange rind.

Heir Apparent

you will need for 1 glass:

4–5 ice cubes	3 parts brandy
3 drops orange bitters or Angostura bitters	3 drops white crème de menthe

1 Put the ice cubes into a glass jug.
2 Shake the bitters over the ice and pour in the brandy.
3 Stir vigorously; strain and pour into a chilled martini glass.
4 Drop in the crème de menthe and serve.

Phipson

you will need for 1 glass:

4–5 ice cubes	3 drops orange bitters or Angostura bitters
juice ½ fresh lime or lemon	1 part Bénédictine
	3 parts brandy

1 Put the ice cubes into a glass jug.
2 Pour in the fruit juice and shake the bitters over the ice.
3 Add the Bénédictine and brandy.
4 Stir vigorously; strain and pour into a chilled martini glass.

Monty Rosa

you will need for 1 glass:

4–5 ice cubes	1 part Cointreau
juice ½ fresh lime or lemon	3 parts brandy

1 Put the ice cubes into a glass jug.
2 Pour the fruit juice, Cointreau and brandy over the ice.
3 Stir vigorously; strain and pour into a chilled martini glass.

Burnt Orange

you will need for 1 glass:

4–5 ice cubes	juice ½ fresh orange (or 2 tablespoons canned, unsweetened juice)
3 drops orange bitters or Angostura bitters	
	3 parts brandy

1 Put the ice cubes into a glass jug.
2 Shake the bitters over the ice.
3 Add the orange juice and brandy.
4 Stir vigorously; strain and pour into a chilled martini glass.

Toulon

you will need for 1 glass:

4–5 ice cubes	1 part Bénédictine
1 part dry French vermouth	3 parts brandy
	1 slice fresh orange rind

1 Put the ice cubes into a glass jug.
2 Pour the vermouth, Bénédictine and brandy over the ice.
3 Stir vigorously; strain and pour into a chilled martini glass.
4 Garnish with the orange rind and serve.

Bergonza

you will need for 1 glass:

4–5 ice cubes
3 drops Angostura
  bitters

1 part sweet Italian
  vermouth
1 part gin
3 parts brandy

1 Put the ice cubes into a glass jug.
2 Shake the bitters over the ice.
3 Add the vermouth, gin and brandy.
4 Stir vigorously; strain and pour into a chilled martini glass.

Star

you will need for 1 glass:

4–5 ice cubes
½ teaspoon sweet
  Italian vermouth
½ teaspoon dry
  French vermouth

juice ½ fresh grapefruit
  (or 2½ tablespoons
  canned, unsweetened
  juice)
1 part gin
3 parts brandy

1 Put the ice cubes into a glass jug.
2 Pour the vermouths, grapefruit juice, gin and brandy over the ice.
3 Stir vigorously; strain and pour into a chilled martini glass.

Prestoman

you will need for 1 glass:

4–5 ice cubes
juice ½ fresh orange
  (or 2 tablespoons
  canned, unsweetened
  juice)

1 part sweet Italian
  vermouth
3 parts brandy
2 drops Pernod

1 Put the ice cubes into a glass jug.
2 Pour the orange juice, vermouth and brandy over the ice.
3 Stir vigorously, strain and pour into a chilled martini glass.
4 At the last moment put the Pernod into the mixture and serve.

Terreno

you will need for 1 glass:

4–5 ice cubes
3 drops Angostura
  bitters

½ teaspoon sugar or
  sugar syrup
2 parts brandy

1 Put the ice cubes into a glass jug.
2 Shake the bitters over the ice.
3 Add the sugar and brandy to the ice.
4 Stir vigorously.
5 Pour without straining into an old-fashioned glass.

The Prince

you will need for 1 glass:

4–5 ice cubes
3 drops orange bitters
  or Angostura bitters

1 teaspoon sugar
3 parts brandy
½ teaspoon white crème
  de menthe

1 Put the ice cubes into a glass jug.
2 Shake the bitters over the ice.
3 Add the sugar and brandy to the ice.
4 Pour without straining into an old-fashioned glass.
5 Pour the white crème de menthe into the mixture and serve.

Freddie

you will need for 1 glass:

4–5 ice cubes
juice ½ fresh lemon
juice ½ fresh orange

3 parts brandy
2 drops white crème
  de menthe

1 Put the ice cubes into a glass jug.
2 Pour the fruit juices and brandy over the ice.
3 Stir vigorously; strain and pour into a chilled martini glass.
4 Add the crème de menthe and serve.

Bradshaw

you will need for 1 glass:

4–5 ice cubes
juice ½ fresh grapefruit
  (or ½ tablespoon
  canned, unsweetened
  juice)
1 part dry French
  vermouth
3 parts brandy

1 Put the ice cubes into a glass jug.
2 Add the grapefruit juice, vermouth and brandy.
3 Stir vigorously; strain and pour into a chilled martini glass.

The Man

you will need for 1 glass:

4–5 ice cubes
3 drops Angostura
  bitters
juice 1 fresh lemon
1 part Bénédictine
3 parts brandy

1 Put the ice cubes into a glass jug.
2 Shake the bitters over the ice.
3 Add the lemon juice, Bénédictine and brandy.
4 Stir vigorously; strain and pour into a chilled martini glass.

Robinson

you will need for 1 glass:

4–5 ice cubes
1 part pineapple juice
1 part dry French
  vermouth
3 parts brandy

1 Put the ice cubes into a glass jug.
2 Pour the pineapple juice, vermouth and brandy over the ice.
3 Stir until frothy.
4 Strain and pour into a sour glass.

Vera Dorian

you will need for 1 glass:

4–5 ice cubes
1 part Amer Picon
½ teaspoon grenadine
1 part dry French
  vermouth
2 parts brandy

1 Put the ice cubes into a glass jug.
2 Pour the Amer Picon, grenadine, vermouth and brandy over the ice.
3 Stir vigorously; strain and pour into a chilled martini glass.

Nico

you will need for 1 glass:

4–5 ice cubes
juice 1 fresh orange
  (or 4 tablespoons
  canned, unsweetened
  juice)
1 part rum
2 parts brandy

1 Put the ice cubes into a glass jug.
2 Pour the orange juice, rum and brandy over the ice.
3 Stir until frothy.
4 Strain and pour into a sour glass.

Depth Bomb

you will need for 1 glass:

4–5 ice cubes
juice 1 fresh lemon
½ teaspoon grenadine
1 part Calvados (apple
  brandy)
2 parts brandy

1 Put the ice cubes into a glass jug.
2 Pour the lemon juice, grenadine, Calvados and brandy over the ice.
3 Stir vigorously; strain and pour into a chilled martini glass.

Mate

you will need for 1 glass:

4–5 ice cubes
½ teaspoon grenadine
juice ½ fresh orange
1 part dry French
  vermouth
3 parts brandy

1 Put the ice cubes into a glass jug.
2 Pour the grenadine, orange juice, vermouth and brandy over the ice.
3 Stir until frothy.
4 Strain and pour into a sour glass.

Klondike

you will need for 1 glass:

4–5 ice cubes
3 drops orange or
  Angostura bitters
1 part dry French
  vermouth
3 parts Calvados (apple
  brandy)

1 Put the ice cubes into a glass jug.
2 Shake the bitters over the ice.
3 Add the vermouth and Calvados.
4 Stir vigorously; strain and pour into a chilled martini glass.

East India

you will need for 1 glass:

4–5 ice cubes
3 drops Angostura
  bitters
½ part pineapple juice
½ part Curaçao
2 parts brandy

1 Put the ice cubes into a glass jug.
2 Shake the bitters over the ice.
3 Add the pineapple juice, Curaçao and brandy.
4 Stir until frothy; strain and pour into a chilled martini glass.

Ciro

you will need for 1 glass:

4–5 ice cubes
3 drops Angostura
  bitters
1 part Curaçao
2 parts brandy

1 Put the ice cubes into a glass jug.
2 Shake the bitters over the ice.
3 Add the Curaçao and brandy.
4 Stir vigorously; strain and pour into a chilled martini glass.

Fascinator

you will need for 1 glass:

4–5 ice cubes
½ teaspoon grenadine
½ teaspoon white
  crème de menthe
1 part gin
2 parts brandy

1 Put the ice cubes into a glass jug.
2 Pour the grenadine, crème de menthe, gin and brandy over the ice.
3 Stir vigorously; strain and pour into a chilled martini glass.

Sidecar

you will need for 1 glass:

4–5 ice cubes
juice 1 fresh lemon
1 part Cointreau
2 parts brandy

1 Put the ice cubes into a glass jug.
2 Pour the lemon juice, Cointreau and brandy over the ice.
3 Stir vigorously; strain and pour into a chilled martini glass.

Tantalus Cocktail

you will need for 1 glass:

4–5 ice cubes
juice 1 fresh lemon
1 part Cointreau
3 parts brandy

1 Put the ice cubes into a glass jug.
2 Pour the lemon juice, Cointreau and brandy over the ice.
3 Stir vigorously; strain and pour into a chilled martini glass.

Esquire

you will need for 1 glass:

4–5 ice cubes
3 drops Angostura
  bitters
1 part gin
2 parts brandy

1 Put the ice cubes into a glass jug.
2 Shake the bitters over the ice.
3 Add the gin and brandy, stir vigorously.
4 Strain and pour into a chilled martini glass.

Drinks that are shaken

Brandy Collins

you will need for 1 glass:

4–5 ice cubes	3 parts brandy
juice 1 fresh lemon	soda water
1 teaspoon sugar or sugar syrup	

1 Put the ice cubes into a cocktail shaker.
2 Pour the lemon juice, sugar and brandy over the ice.
3 Shake until a frost forms then pour, without straining, into a collins glass.
4 Top with soda water, stir gently and serve.

Brandy Rickey

you will need for 1 glass:

4–5 ice cubes	soda water
juice 1 fresh lime	1 maraschino cherry
½ teaspoon sugar	(optional)
3 parts brandy	hull ½ fresh lime

1 Put the ice cubes into a cocktail shaker.
2 Pour the lime juice, sugar and brandy over the ice.
3 Shake until a frost forms and pour, without straining, into a collins glass.
4 Drop in the cherry and the hull of the lime.
5 Top with soda and serve.

Brandy Punch

you will need for 1 glass:

4–5 ice cubes	3 parts brandy
1 teaspoon sugar or sugar syrup	3 parts milk
	ground nutmeg

1 Put the ice cubes into a cocktail shaker.
2 Pour the sugar, brandy and milk over the ice.
3 Shake until a frost forms.
4 Pour without straining into a lowball glass.
5 Sprinkle a little ground nutmeg on top and serve.

Tinker

you will need for 1 glass:

4–5 ice cubes	3 parts brandy
juice ½ fresh lime or lemon	dry ginger ale

1 Put the ice cubes into a cocktail shaker.
2 Pour in the fruit juice and brandy.
3 Shake until a frost forms.
4 Pour, without straining, into a highball glass.
5 Top with dry ginger ale and serve.

Brandy Fizz

you will need for 1 glass:

4–5 ice cubes	1 part yellow Chartreuse
juice 1 fresh lemon	2 parts brandy
1 teaspoon sugar or sugar syrup	soda water

1 Put the ice cubes into a cocktail shaker.
2 Pour the lemon juice, sugar, Chartreuse and brandy over the ice.
3 Shake until a frost forms.
4 Pour without straining into a collins glass.
5 Top with soda, stir a bit and serve.

Brandy Daisy

you will need for 1 glass:

4–5 ice cubes	1 slice fresh orange
juice 1 fresh lemon	1 slice lemon
½ teaspoon grenadine	1 maraschino cherry
2 parts brandy	

1 Put the ice cubes into a cocktail shaker.
2 Pour the lemon juice, grenadine and brandy over the ice.
3 Shake until a frost forms.
4 Pour without shaking into a lowball glass.
5 Garnish with fruit and serve.

French '75

you will need for 1 glass:

4–5 ice cubes	2 parts brandy
juice 1 fresh lemon	champagne
3 drops Angostura bitters	

1 Put the ice cubes into a cocktail shaker.
2 Pour the lemon juice, bitters and brandy over the ice.
3 Shake until a frost forms.
4 Strain and pour into a chilled champagne glass.
5 Top with champagne and serve.

Thunder

you will need for 1 glass:

4–5 ice cubes   3 parts brandy
1 egg yolk   ground black pepper
1 teaspoon sugar or
  sugar syrup

1 Put the ice cubes into a cocktail shaker.
2 Pour the egg yolk, sugar and brandy over the ice.
3 Sprinkle a very little ground pepper on to the mixture.
4 Shake until a frost forms.
5 Strain and pour into a lowball glass.

Bosom Caresser

you will need for 1 glass:

4–5 ice cubes   ½ part Curaçao
1 egg yolk   ½ part Madeira
½ teaspoon grenadine   2 parts brandy

1 Put the ice cubes into a cocktail shaker.
2 Pour the egg yolk, grenadine, Curaçao, Madeira and brandy over the ice.
3 Shake until a frost forms; strain and pour into a chilled champagne glass.

Quencher

you will need for 1 glass:

4–5 ice cubes   1 teaspoon sugar
1 egg white   3 parts brandy
3 drops Angostura   dry ginger ale
  bitters

1 Put the ice cubes into a cocktail shaker.
2 Pour the white of the egg, the bitters, sugar and brandy over the ice.
3 Shake until a frost forms; pour without straining in a highball glass.
4 Top with dry ginger ale and serve.

Coffee

you will need for 1 glass:

4–5 ice cubes   1 part port
1 egg yolk   3 parts brandy
1 teaspoon sugar

1 Put the ice cubes into a cocktail shaker.
2 Pour the egg yolk, sugar, port and brandy over the ice.
3 Shake until a frost forms.
4 Strain and pour into a lowball glass.

Brandy Sour

you will need for 1 glass:

4–5 ice cubes   3 parts brandy
3 drops Angostura   1 teaspoon sugar or
  bitters   sugar syrup
juice 1 fresh lemon

1 Put the ice cubes into a cocktail shaker.
2 Shake the bitters, the lemon juice, sugar and brandy over the ice.
3 Shake until a frost forms.
4 Strain and pour into a sour glass.

Bobby Jones

you will need for 1 glass:

4–5 ice cubes   1 part crème de cacao
juice 1 fresh lemon   3 parts brandy
½ teaspoon grenadine

1 Put the ice cubes into a cocktail shaker.
2 Pour the lemon juice, grenadine, crème de cacao and brandy over the ice.
3 Shake until a frost forms.
4 Strain and pour into a sour glass.

Discovery

you will need for 1 glass:

4–5 ice cubes   ½ part Amer Picon
3 drops Angostura   1 part Curaçao
  bitters   1 part sweet Italian
½ teaspoon sugar or   vermouth
  sugar syrup   3 parts brandy

1 Put the ice cubes into a cocktail shaker.
2 Shake the bitters and pour sugar, Amer Picon, Curaçao, vermouth and brandy over the ice.

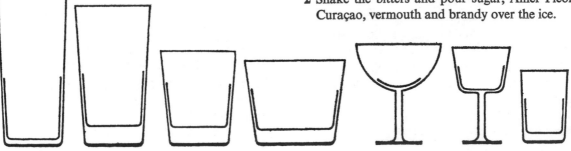

3 Shake until a frost forms.
4 Strain and pour into a sour glass.

Glad Eye Cocktail

you will need for 1 glass:

4–5 ice cubes	2 drops orange bitters
2 drops Angostura bitters	½ teaspoon grenadine
	3 parts brandy

1 Put the ice cubes into a cocktail shaker.
2 Pour the bitters, grenadine and brandy over the ice.
3 Shake until a frost forms.
4 Strain and pour into a sour glass.

Stinger

you will need for 1 glass:

4–5 ice cubes	3 parts brandy
1 part white crème de menthe	

1 Put the ice cubes into a cocktail shaker.
2 Pour the crème de menthe and brandy over the ice.
3 Shake until a frost forms.
4 Strain and pour into a chilled martini glass.

Jack Rose

you will need for 1 glass:

4–5 ice cubes	½ teaspoon grenadine
juice 1 fresh lime or lemon	3 parts Calvados (apple brandy)

1 Put the ice cubes into a cocktail shaker.
2 Pour the fruit juice, grenadine and brandy over the ice.
3 Shake until a frost forms.
4 Strain and pour into a chilled martini glass.

Brandy Alexander

you will need for 1 glass:

4–5 ice cubes	1 part crème de cacao
1 part cream	3 parts brandy

1 Put the ice cubes into a cocktail shaker.
2 Pour the cream, crème de cacao and brandy over the ice.
3 Shake until a frost forms.
4 Strain and pour into a sour glass.

Brandt

you will need for 1 glass:

4–5 ice cubes	3 parts brandy
3 drops Angostura bitters	1 slice fresh lemon rind
1 part white crème de menthe	

1 Put the ice cubes into a cocktail shaker.
2 Pour the bitters, crème de menthe and brandy over the ice.
3 Shake until a frost forms.
4 Strain and pour into a chilled martini glass.
5 Twist the lemon rind over the mixture, drop it in and serve.

Cuban Cocktail

you will need for 1 glass:

4–5 ice cubes	1 part apricot brandy
juice ½ fresh lime or lemon	2 parts brandy

1 Put the ice cubes into a cocktail shaker.
2 Pour the fruit juice, apricot brandy and brandy over the ice.
3 Shake until a frost forms.
4 Strain and pour into a chilled martini glass.

Between the Sheets

you will need for 1 glass:

4–5 ice cubes	1 part thin cream
3 drops Angostura bitters	1 part crème de cacao
	2 parts brandy
1 teaspoon sugar or sugar syrup	1 slice fresh lemon rind

1 Put the ice cubes into a cocktail shaker.
2 Pour the bitters, the sugar, cream, crème de cacao and brandy over the ice.
3 Shake until a frost forms.
4 Strain and pour into a sour glass.
5 Twist the lemon rind over the drink, drop it in and serve.

In the Clear

you will need for 1 glass:

4–5 ice cubes	½ teaspoon sugar or sugar syrup
juice ½ fresh lemon	½ teaspoon grenadine
1 egg white	2 parts brandy

1 Put the ice cubes into a cocktail shaker.
2 Pour the lemon juice, sugar, grenadine, egg white and brandy over the ice.
3 Shake until a frost forms.
4 Strain and pour into a sour glass.

Brandy Flip

you will need for 1 glass:

4–5 ice cubes
1 egg
½ teaspoon sugar or
    sugar syrup
2 parts brandy

1 Put the ice cubes into a cocktail shaker.
2 Pour the egg, sugar and brandy over the ice.
3 Shake until a frost forms.
4 Strain and pour into sour glass.

St. Kitts

you will need for 1 glass:

4–5 ice cubes
juice ½ fresh grapefruit
    (or 2½ tablespoons
    canned, unsweetened
    juice)
1 part dry French
    vermouth
3 parts brandy
1 maraschino cherry
    (optional)

1 Put the ice cubes into a cocktail shaker.
2 Pour the grapefruit juice, vermouth and brandy over the ice.
3 Shake until a frost forms.
4 Strain and pour into a chilled martini glass.
5 Drop in the cherry and serve.

Coffee No. 2

you will need for 1 glass:

4–5 ice cubes
1 well beaten egg yolk
½ teaspoon Curaçao
3 drops Angostura
    bitters
1 part port
2 parts brandy
ground nutmeg

1 Put the ice cubes into a cocktail shaker.
2 Pour the egg yolk, Curaçao and bitters over the ice and add the port and brandy.
3 Shake until a frost forms.
4 Strain and pour into a sour glass.
5 Sprinkle the top with a little nutmeg and serve.

Gymkhana

4–5 ice cubes
3 drops Angostura
    bitters
juice 1 fresh lime or
    lemon
½ part Curaçao
1 part ginger wine
1 part brandy

1 Put the ice cubes into a cocktail shaker.
2 Pour the bitters, fruit juice, Curaçao, ginger wine and brandy over the ice.
3 Shake until a frost forms.
4 Strain and pour into a sour glass.

Drinks for a heatwave

Sangria

you will need for 1 glass:

4–5 ice cubes
3 drops Angostura
    bitters
juice 1 fresh lemon
juice 2 fresh oranges
    (or 8 tablespoons
    canned, unsweetened
    juice)
2 parts red wine
    (Burgundy or Spanish
    Tinto)
3 parts brandy
1 slice fresh lemon
1 slice orange
1 fresh cherry

1 Put the ice cubes into a glass jug.
2 Shake the bitters over the ice.
3 Add the fruit juices, wine and brandy.
4 Stir vigorously, until well chilled.
5 Pour without straining into a collins glass.
6 Garnish with fresh fruit and serve.

Brandy Julep

you will need for 1 glass:

3 sprigs young mint
1 teaspoon sugar or
    sugar syrup
cracked ice
3 parts brandy

1 Put the mint and sugar into the base of an iced silver mug or collins glass.
2 Swirl this round so that the mixture spreads along the sides.
3 Pack cracked ice into the mug or glass.
4 Pour in the brandy and stir gently.
5 Add more ice, stir until a heavy frost forms.
6 Wrap in a table napkin and serve.

Brandy Mist

you will need for 1 glass:

crushed ice
1 sprig young mint
    leaves
2 parts brandy

1 Fill an old-fashioned glass with crushed ice.
2 Garnish with mint and pour in the brandy.
3 Stir lightly and serve.

Vodka Drinks

Genuine vodka is a distilled spirit made mostly of barley, malt and rye. It is a neutral spirit, now more often made from maize and potatoes. Because it is colourless and without a pronounced flavour it has become very popular in making mixed drinks.

A word of caution: because one is not aware of a flavour, some people, on first acquaintance with vodka mixed-drinks, can be inclined to drink too much.

Drinks that are stirred

Vodka and Water

you will need for 1 glass:

2–3 ice cubes	water
1 measure vodka	1 slice fresh lemon

1 Put the ice cubes into a highball glass.
2 Pour the vodka over the ice.
3 Add water to taste.
4 Garnish with the lemon.
5 Stir and serve.

Vodka Sazerac

you will need for 1 glass:

1 cube sugar	3 drops Pernod
2 drops Peychaud bitters or Angostura bitters	2–0 ice cubes
	2 parts vodka

1 Put the cube of sugar into the base of an old-fashioned glass.
2 Shake the bitters on to the sugar.
3 Add the Pernod, and with a spoon swirl the mixture about so that it clings to the side of the glass.
4 Put in the ice cubes and pour in the vodka.
5 Stir gently and serve.

Moscow Mule

you will need for 1 glass:

3 ice cubes	1 slice fresh lemon
2 parts vodka	1 slice fresh cucumber
ginger beer	

1 Put the ice cubes into a copper mug or an old-fashioned glass.
2 Pour the vodka and as much ginger beer as desired over the ice.
3 Garnish with the lemon and the cucumber, stir gently and serve.

Vodka and French

you will need for 1 glass:

1 part dry French vermouth	2 parts vodka

1 Pour the vermouth into a sherry glass.
2 Add the vodka.
3 Stir gently and serve.

Vodka and Italian

you will need for 1 glass:

1 part sweet Italian   2 parts vodka
  vermouth

1 Pour the vermouth into a sherry glass.
2 Add the vodka.
3 Stir gently and serve.

Vodka and Tonic

you will need for 1 glass:

2–3 ice cubes   tonic water
1 part vodka   1 slice fresh lemon

1 Put the ice cubes into a highball glass.
2 Pour the vodka and tonic water, to taste, over
  the ice.
3 Garnish with lemon and serve.

Vodka and Coke

you will need for 1 glass:

2–3 ice cubes   Coca Cola
1 part vodka   1 slice fresh lemon

1 Put the ice cubes into a highball glass.
2 Pour the vodka and Coca Cola, to taste, over
  the ice.
3 Garnish with the lemon.
4 Stir gently and serve.

Vodka Salty Dog

you will need for 1 glass:

2–3 ice cubes   1 part vodka
juice ½ fresh grapefruit pinch salt
  (or 2½ tablespoons
  canned, unsweetened
  juice)

1 Put the ice cubes into a highball glass.
2 Pour the grapefruit juice and vodka over the
  ice.
3 Add the salt.
4 Stir well and serve.

Vodka and Pineapple

you will need for 1 glass:

2–3 ice cubes   1 maraschino cherry
1 part vodka   (optional)
2–2½ parts unsweetened
  pineapple juice

1 Put the ice cubes into a highball glass.
2 Pour the vodka and pineapple juice over the
  ice.
3 Stir gently.
4 Drop in the cherry and serve.

Screwdriver

you will need for 1 glass:

2–3 ice cubes   Angostura bitters
1 part vodka   (optional)
juice 1 fresh orange
  (or 4 tablespoons
  canned, unsweetened
  juice)

1 Put the ice cubes into a highball glass.
2 Pour the vodka and orange juice over the ice.
3 Add the bitters if used.
4 Stir gently; serve.

Vodka Rickey

you will need for 1 glass:

3–4 ice cubes   flesh ½ lime
½ teaspoon sugar or   soda water
  sugar syrup   1 sprig fresh mint
juice 1 fresh lime   1 maraschino cherry
3 parts vodka

1 Put the ice cubes into a collins glass.
2 Pour the sugar, lime juice and vodka over the
  ice.
3 Add soda water to taste.
4 Drop in the flesh of the lime.
5 Garnish with the mint and cherry.
6 Stir once and serve.

Vodka and Pink

you will need for 1 glass:

2–3 drops Angostura bitters   1 part vodka
ice water

1 Splash the bitters into a sour glass.
2 Swirl the glass until the bitters spread along the sides.
3 Pour in the vodka and ice water to taste.

Vodka Martini

you will need for 1 glass:

4–5 ice cubes   3 parts vodka
1 part dry French vermouth   1 Spanish olive

1 Put the ice cubes into a glass jug.
2 Pour the vermouth and vodka over the ice.
3 Stir vigorously, without splashing.
4 Strain and pour into a chilled martini glass.
5 Drop in the olive and serve.

Dry Vodka Martini

you will need for 1 glass:

5–6 ice cubes   4 parts vodka
1 part dry French vermouth   1 slice fresh lemon rind

1 Put the ice cubes into a glass jug.
2 Pour the vermouth and vodka over the ice.
3 Stir vigorously, without splashing.
4 Rub the lemon rind around the rim of a chilled martini glass.
5 Stir the mixture again, strain and pour into a glass.
6 Twist the lemon rind over the drink, drop it in and serve.

Extra Dry Vodka Martini

you will need for 1 glass:

5–6 ice cubes   5 parts vodka
1 part dry French vermouth   1 pickled pearl onion

1 Put the ice cubes into a glass jug.
2 Pour the vermouth and vodka over the ice.
3 Stir vigorously, without splashing.
4 Strain and pour into a chilled martini glass.
5 Spear a small onion with a toothpick and put it into the drink.

New Orleans Dry Vodka Martini

you will need for 1 glass:

5–6 ice cubes   1 part dry French vermouth
3 drops Pernod   3 parts vodka

1 Put the ice cubes into a glass jug.
2 Shake the Pernod over the ice.
3 Add the vermouth and vodka.
4 Stir vigorously, without splashing.
5 Strain and pour into a chilled martini glass.

Vodka Gibson

you will need for 1 glass:

5–6 ice cubes   5 parts vodka
1 part extra dry sherry   1 pickled pearl onion

1 Put the ice cubes into a glass jug.
2 Pour the sherry and vodka over the ice.
3 Stir vigorously, without splashing.
4 Strain and pour into a chilled martini glass.
5 Spear a pickled onion and drop it in.

Vodka Perfect

you will need for 1 glass:

4–5 ice cubes   1 part sweet Italian vermouth
1 part dry French vermouth   3 parts vodka
1 slice fresh lemon rind

1 Put the ice cubes into a glass jug.
2 Pour the vermouths and vodka over the ice.
3 Stir vigorously, without splashing.
4 Strain and pour into a chilled martini glass.
5 Twist the lemon rind over the mixture and drop it in.

Vodka Dubonnet

you will need for 1 glass:

4–5 ice cubes   2 parts vodka
1 part Dubonnet   1 slice fresh lemon rind

1 Put the ice cubes into a glass jug.
2 Pour the Dubonnet and vodka over the ice.
3 Stir vigorously, strain and pour into a chilled martini glass.
4 Twist the lemon rind over the drink and drop it in.

Vodka Gimlet

you will need for 1 glass:

4–5 ice cubes   3 parts vodka
1 part bottled lime juice

1 Put the ice cubes into a glass jug.
2 Pour the lime juice and vodka over the ice.
3 Stir vigorously, strain and pour into a chilled martini glass.

Vodka Zaza

you will need for 1 glass:

4–5 ice cubes   1 part Dubonnet
3 drops orange or   2 parts vodka
  Angostura bitters

1 Put the ice cubes into a glass jug.
2 Shake the bitters over the ice and add the Dubonnet and vodka.
3 Stir vigorously; strain and pour into a chilled martini glass.

Long drinks that are shaken

Vodka Collins

you will need for 1 glass:

4–5 ice cubes   3 parts vodka
1 teaspoon sugar or   soda water
  sugar syrup   1 slice fresh lemon
juice 1 fresh lemon   1 sprig fresh mint

1 Put the ice cubes into a cocktail shaker.
2 Pour the sugar, lemon juice and vodka over the ice.
3 Shake until a frost forms.
4 Pour without straining, into a collins glass.
5 Top with soda water.
6 Garnish with the fruit and mint.
7 Stir once and serve.

Vodka Silver Fizz

you will need for 1 glass:

4–5 ice cubes   juice 1 fresh lemon
½ teaspoon sugar or   3 parts vodka
  sugar syrup   soda water
1 egg white

1 Put the ice cubes into a cocktail shaker.
2 Pour the sugar, lemon juice, egg white and vodka over the ice.
3 Shake until a frost forms.
4 Pour without straining into a highball glass.
5 Top with soda and serve.

Down-under Fizz

you will need for 1 glass:

4–5 ice cubes   ½ teaspoon grenadine
juice 1 fresh lemon   3 parts vodka
juice ½ fresh orange (or   soda water
  2 tablespoons canned,
  unsweetened juice)

1 Put the ice cubes into a cocktail shaker.
2 Pour the fruit juices, grenadine and vodka over the ice.
3 Shake until a frost forms; pour, without straining into a collins glass.
4 Top with soda and serve.

Ramos Vodka Fizz

you will need for 1 glass:

4–5 ice cubes   3 drops Angostura
juice 1 fresh lemon   bitters
1 part thin cream   2 parts vodka
1 egg white

1 Put the ice cubes into a cocktail shaker.
2 Pour the lemon juice, cream, egg white, bitters and vodka over the ice.
3 Shake until a frost forms, and pour, without straining, into a lowball glass.

Vodka Twister Fizz

you will need for 1 glass:

4–5 ice cubes
juice 1 fresh lemon
½ teaspoon sugar or
   sugar syrup
1 egg white

3 drops Pernod
3 parts vodka
dry ginger ale

1 Put the ice cubes into a cocktail shaker.
2 Pour the lemon juice, sugar, egg white, Pernod and vodka over the ice.
3 Shake until a frost forms.
4 Pour without straining into a highball glass.
5 Top with dry ginger ale.
6 Stir once or twice and serve.

Opossum

you will need for 1 glass:

4–5 ice cubes
juice 1 fresh lemon
juice ½ fresh orange
   (or 2 tablespoons
   canned, unsweetened
   juice)

½ teaspoon grenadine
3 drops Angostura
   bitters
3 parts vodka
soda water
1 slice fresh orange

1 Put the ice cubes into a cocktail shaker.
2 Pour the fruit juices, grenadine, bitters and vodka over the ice.
3 Shake until a frost forms.
4 Pour without straining into a lowball glass.
5 Top with soda water and serve.
6 Garnish with orange.

Vodka Sling

you will need for 1 glass:

4–5 ice cubes
juice ½ fresh lemon
1 part cherry brandy

3 parts vodka
soda water

1 Put the ice cubes into a cocktail shaker.
2 Pour the lemon juice, cherry brandy and vodka over the ice.
3 Shake until a frost forms.
4 Pour without straining into a lowball glass.
5 Top with soda and serve.

Heron Island Vodka Sling

you will need for 1 glass:

4–5 ice cubes
juice ½ fresh lemon
juice ½ fresh orange
   (or 2 tablespoons
   canned, unsweetened
   juice)

1 part brandy
3 parts vodka
3 drops Angostura
   bitters
soda water

1 Put the ice cubes into a cocktail shaker.
2 Pour the fruit juices, brandy, vodka and bitters over the ice.
3 Shake until a frost forms.
4 Pour without straining into a highball glass.
5 Top with soda and serve.

Bloody Mary

you will need for 1 glass:

4–5 ice cubes
juice ½ fresh lemon
2 drops Angostura
   bitters
2 drops Worcester
   sauce

1 drop Tobasco sauce
pinch salt and pepper
2 parts thick tomato
   juice
2 parts vodka

1 Put the ice cubes into a cocktail shaker.
2 Pour the lemon juice, bitters, Worcester sauce, Tobasco sauce, salt and pepper, tomato juice and vodka over the ice.
3 Shake until a frost forms.
4 Strain and pour into a lowball glass.

Short drinks that are shaken

Vodka Sour

you will need for 1 glass:

4–5 ice cubes
juice 1 fresh lemon

½ teaspoon sugar or
    sugar syrup
3 parts vodka

1 Put the ice cubes into a cocktail shaker.
2 Pour the lemon juice, sugar and vodka over the ice.
3 Shake until a frost forms.
4 Strain and pour into a sour glass.

Vodka Bronx

you will need for 1 glass:

4–5 ice cubes
1 part dry French
    vermouth
1 part sweet Italian
    vermouth

juice ½ fresh orange
    (or 2 tablespoons
    canned, unsweetened
    juice)
3 parts vodka

1 Put the ice cubes into a cocktail shaker.
2 Pour the vermouths, orange juice and vodka over the ice.
3 Shake until a frost forms.
4 Strain and pour into a chilled martini glass.

Sutherland

you will need for 1 glass:

4–5 ice cubes
juice 1 fresh lemon

1 part dry French
    vermouth
3 parts vodka

1 Put the ice cubes into a cocktail shaker.
2 Pour the lemon juice, vermouth and vodka over the ice.
3 Shake until a frost forms.
4 Strain and pour into a chilled martini glass.

Macbelius

you will need for 1 glass:

4–5 ice cubes
1 part dry French
    vermouth

1 part cherry brandy
3 parts vodka

1 Put the ice cubes into a cocktail shaker.
2 Pour the vermouth, cherry brandy and vodka over the ice.
3 Shake until a frost forms.
4 Strain and pour into a chilled martini glass.

Surf Rider

you will need for 1 glass:

4–5 ice cubes
juice ½ fresh lemon
juice 1 fresh orange
    (or 4 tablespoons
    canned, unsweetened
    juice)

½ teaspoon grenadine
1 part sweet Italian
    vermouth
3 parts vodka

1 Put the ice cubes into a cocktail shaker.
2 Pour the fruit juices, grenadine, vermouth and vodka over the ice.
3 Shake until a frost forms.
4 Strain and pour into a sour glass.

Hawaiian Vodka

you will need for 1 glass:

4–5 ice cubes
1 part pineapple juice
juice 1 fresh lemon

juice 1 fresh orange
    (or 4 tablespoons
    canned, unsweetened
    juice)
1 teaspoon grenadine
3 parts vodka

1 Put the ice cubes into a cocktail shaker.
2 Pour the fruit juices, grenadine and vodka over the ice.
3 Shake until a frost forms; strain and pour into a sour glass.

Vodka Hula

you will need for 1 glass:

4–5 ice cubes
juice 1 fresh lemon
1 part pineapple juice

½ part dry French
    vermouth
3 parts vodka

1 Put the ice cubes into a cocktail shaker.
2 Pour the fruit juices, vermouth and vodka over the ice.
3 Shake until a frost forms; strain and pour into a sour glass.

Banjo

you will need for 1 glass:

4–5 ice cubes
1 part pineapple juice
juice ½ fresh grapefruit
  (or 2½ tablespoons
  canned, unsweetened
  juice)
1 teaspoon sugar or
  sugar syrup
3 parts vodka
1 maraschino cherry

1 Put the ice cubes into a cocktail shaker.
2 Pour the fruit juices, sugar, and vodka over the ice.
3 Shake until a frost forms; strain and pour into a sour glass.
4 Add the cherry and serve.

Seafoam

you will need for 1 glass:

4–5 ice cubes
juice 1 fresh lime or
  lemon
½ teaspoon sugar or
  sugar syrup
1 egg white
3 parts vodka

1 Put the ice cubes into a cocktail shaker.
2 Pour the fruit juice, sugar, egg white and vodka over the ice.
3 Shake until a frost forms; strain and pour into a sour glass.

Pink Seafoam

you will need for 1 glass:

4–5 ice cubes
juice 1 fresh lime or
  lemon
1 teaspoon grenadine
1 egg white
3 parts vodka

1 Put the ice cubes into a cocktail shaker.
2 Pour the fruit juice, grenadine, egg white and vodka over the ice.
3 Shake until a frost forms; strain and pour into a sour glass.

Sadie Thompson

you will need for 1 glass:

4–5 ice cubes
juice 1 grapefruit (or
  5 tablespoons
  canned, unsweetened
  juice)
½ teaspoon sugar or
  sugar syrup
2 parts vodka
3 drops Pernod

1 Put the ice cubes into a cocktail shaker.
2 Pour the grapefruit juice, sugar, vodka and Pernod over the ice.
3 Shake until a frost forms; strain and pour into a chilled martini glass.

Alex

you will need for 1 glass:

4–5 ice cubes
juice 1 fresh grapefruit
  (or 5 tablespoons
  canned, unsweetened
  juice)
1 part Calvados (apple
  brandy)
2 parts vodka

1 Put the ice cubes into a cocktail shaker.
2 Pour the grapefruit juice, Calvados and vodka over the ice.
3 Shake until a frost forms; strain and pour into a sour glass.

Yokohama

you will need for 1 glass:

4–5 ice cubes
juice 1 fresh orange
  (or 4 tablespoons
  canned, unsweetened
  juice)
½ teaspoon grenadine
3 drops Pernod
3 parts vodka

1 Put the ice cubes into a cocktail shaker.
2 Pour the orange juice, grenadine, Pernod and the vodka over the ice.
3 Shake until a frost forms; strain and pour into a chilled martini glass.

Some of the more exotic drinks

Haven

you will need for 1 glass:

2–3 ice cubes	1 part Pernod
3–4 drops grenadine	1 part vodka

1 Put the ice cubes into an old-fashioned glass.
2 Put the grenadine over the ice.
3 Pour in the Pernod and vodka.
4 Stir gently and serve.

Vodka Negroni

you will need for 1 glass:

3 ice cubes	3 parts vodka
½ part bitter Campari	1 slice fresh orange
1 part sweet Italian vermouth	soda water

1 Put the ice cubes into a lowball glass.
2 Pour the Campari, vermouth and vodka over the ice.
3 Stir gently to mix.
4 Top with soda water.
5 Garnish with the orange and serve.

Gary

you will need for 1 glass:

2–3 ice cubes	2 parts vodka
1 part sweet Italian vermouth	½ teaspoon grenadine
¼ part Amer Picon	1 slice fresh orange

1 Put the ice cubes into a lowball glass.
2 Pour the vermouth, Amer Picon, vodka and grenadine over the ice.
3 Stir evenly to mix and serve garnished with orange.

Xantippe

you will need for 1 glass:

4–5 ice cubes	1 part yellow Chartreuse
1 part cherry brandy	2 parts vodka

1 Put the ice cubes into a glass jug.
2 Pour the brandy, Chartreuse and vodka over the ice.
3 Stir vigorously; strain and pour into a chilled martini glass.

Perth

you will need for 1 glass:

4–5 ice cubes	½ teaspoon grenadine
juice 1 fresh lemon	3 parts vodka
1 part sweet Italian vermouth	

1 Put the ice cubes into a glass jug.
2 Pour the lemon juice, vermouth, grenadine and vodka over the ice.
3 Stir gently; strain and pour into a chilled martini glass.

Fresh Wind

you will need for 1 glass:

4–5 ice cubes	juice ½ fresh grapefruit
1 part dry French vermouth	½ teaspoon Cointreau
	3 parts vodka

1 Put the ice cubes into a glass jug.
2 Pour the vermouth, grapefruit juice, Cointreau and vodka over the ice.
3 Stir gently; strain and pour into a chilled martini glass.

King Vodka

you will need for 1 glass:

4–5 ice cubes	1 part sweet Italian
3 drops orange bitters	vermouth
3 drops Angostura	3 parts vodka
bitters	

1 Put the ice cubes into a glass jug.
2 Pour the bitters, vermouth and vodka over the ice.
3 Stir gently, strain and pour into a chilled martini glass.

Oratorio

you will need for 1 glass:

4–5 ice cubes	1 part Dubonnet
½ part Curaçao	2 parts vodka

1 Put the ice cubes into a glass jug.
2 Pour the Curaçao, Dubonnet and vodka over the ice.
3 Stir vigorously; strain and pour into a chilled martini glass.

Inspiration

you will need for 1 glass:

4–5 ice cubes	2 parts vodka
½ part Bénédictine	1 slice fresh lemon rind
½ part dry French	
vermouth	

1 Put the ice cubes into a glass jug.
2 Pour the Bénédictine, vermouth and vodka over the ice.
3 Stir vigorously; strain and pour into a chilled martini glass.

San Luis

you will need for 1 glass:

4–5 ice cubes	1 part sweet Italian
3 drops Angostura	vermouth
bitters	3 parts vodka
3 drops Pernod	
1 part dry French	
vermouth	

1 Put the ice cubes into a glass jug.
2 Shake the bitters and Pernod over the ice.
3 Add the vermouths and vodka.
4 Stir vigorously; strain and pour into a chilled martini glass.

Cygnet

you will need for 1 glass:

4–5 ice cubes	1 part dry French
juice 1 fresh lime or	vermouth
lemon	3 parts vodka
3 drops Pernod	
3 drops Angostura	
bitters	

1 Put the ice cubes into a glass jug.
2 Pour in the fruit juice, Pernod, bitters, vermouth and vodka.
3 Stir vigorously; strain and pour into a chilled martini glass.

Federation

you will need for 1 glass:

4–5 ice cubes	1 part port
3 drops orange bitters	2 parts vodka
or Angostura bitters	

1 Put the ice cubes into a glass jug.
2 Shake the bitters over the ice.
3 Add the port and vodka.
4 Stir vigorously; strain and pour into a chilled martini glass.

Port Elizabeth

you will need for 1 glass:

4–5 ice cubes	1 part dry French
3 drops Angostura	vermouth
bitters	1 part sweet Italian
½ teaspoon white	vermouth
Curaçao	3 parts vodka

1 Put the ice cubes into a glass jug.
2 Shake the bitters and pour the Curaçao, vermouths and vodka over the ice.
3 Stir vigorously; strain and pour into a chilled martini glass.

Combined Forces

you will need for 1 glass:

4–5 ice cubes	1 part dry French
½ fresh lemon	vermouth
½ teaspoon white	2 parts vodka
Curaçao	

1 Put the ice cubes into a glass jug.
2 Pour the lemon juice, white Curaçao, vermouth and vodka over the ice.
3 Stir vigorously; strain and pour into a chilled martini glass.

Whitehorn

you will need for 1 glass:

4–5 ice cubes
2 drops Angostura bitters
1 part sweet Italian vermouth

3 parts vodka
1 slice fresh lemon rind

1 Put the ice cubes into a glass jug.
2 Shake the bitters and pour the vermouth and vodka over the ice.
3 Stir vigorously; strain and pour into a chilled martini glass.
4 Twist the lemon rind over the drink and drop it in.

Leolin

you will need for 1 glass:

4–5 ice cubes
juice 1 fresh lime or lemon

2 drops Peychaud or Angostura bitters
1 part apricot brandy
3 parts vodka

1 Put the ice cubes into a glass jug.
2 Pour the fruit juice, bitters, apricot brandy and vodka over the ice.
3 Stir vigorously; strain and pour into a chilled martini glass.

Pale Rose

you will need for 1 glass:

4–5 ice cubes
1 part Grand Marnier

3 parts vodka

1 Put the ice cubes into a glass jug.
2 Pour the Grand Marnier and vodka over the ice.
3 Stir evenly; strain and pour into a chilled martini glass.

Drizzler

you will need for 1 glass:

4–5 ice cubes
1 part Curaçao
1 part kümmel

2 parts Vielle Curé
3 parts vodka

1 Put the ice cubes into a glass jug.
2 Pour in the Curaçao, kümmel, Vielle Curé and vodka.
3 Stir evenly; strain and pour into a chilled martini glass.

Davey-davey

you will need for 1 glass:

4–5 ice cubes
juice ½ fresh grapefruit (or 2½ tablespoons canned, unsweetened juice)

1 part Calvados (apple brandy)
2 parts vodka

1 Put the ice cubes into a glass jug.
2 Pour the fruit juice, Calvados and vodka over the ice.
3 Stir vigorously; strain and pour into a chilled martini glass.

Herbert Lee

you will need for 1 glass:

4–5 ice cubes
1 part Calvados (apple brandy)

2 parts vodka
1 teaspoon crème de Cassis

1 Put the ice cubes into a glass jug.
2 Pour the Calvados, vodka and crème de Cassis over the ice.
3 Stir vigorously; strain and pour into a chilled martini glass.

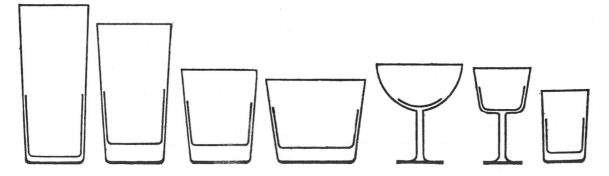

Drinks for a heatwave

Cherry Vodka Julep

you will need for 1 glass:

ice
juice ½ fresh lemon
1 teaspoon sugar or
  sugar syrup
1 teaspoon maraschino
  syrup or grenadine

1 part cherry brandy
1 part sloe gin
3 parts vodka
1 slice fresh lemon
1 slice orange

1 Fill a collins glass with chopped ice.
2 Put 3 or 4 ice cubes into a glass jug.
3 Pour the lemon juice, sugar, maraschino, brandy, vodka and gin over the ice.
4 Stir vigorously.
5 Strain and pour into the ice-filled glass.
6 Garnish with fresh fruit and serve.

Head-over-Heels

you will need for 1 glass:

4–5 ice cubes
juice 1 fresh lime or
  lemon
1 teaspoon sugar or
  sugar syrup

3 parts vodka
3 drops Angostura
  bitters
Champagne

1 Put the ice cubes into a cocktail shaker.
2 Pour the fruit juice, sugar, vodka and bitters over the ice.
3 Shake until a frost begins to form.
4 Pour without straining into a highball glass.
5 Top with Champagne and serve.

Vodka Cup

you will need for 1 glass:

1 sprig fresh mint
1 teaspoon sugar or
  sugar syrup

crushed ice
juice ½ fresh lemon
3 parts vodka

This drink is best served in a silver mug.

1 Put the mint and sugar into the mug.
2 Stir them together, bruising the mint.
3 Fill the mug with crushed ice.
4 Pour the lemon juice and vodka over the minted ice.
5 Stir until a heavy frost forms; wrap with a table napkin and serve.

The Widower

you will need for 1 glass:

4–5 ice cubes
juice fresh lemon
1 teaspoon sugar or
  sugar syrup

1 part dark rum
4 parts vodka
Champagne

1 Put the ice cubes into a cocktail shaker.
2 Pour the lemon juice, sugar, rum and vodka over the ice.
3 Shake until a frost forms; strain and pour into an ice-filled champagne glass.
4 Top with Champagne and serve.

Cavendish

you will need for 1 glass:

chopped ice
2 drops Angostura
  bitters

2 parts vodka
Champagne
1 slice fresh lemon rind

1 Fill a highball glass with chopped ice.
2 Shake the bitters on to the ice.
3 Pour in the vodka and top with Champagne.
4 Twist the fresh lemon rind over the mixture, drop it in and serve.

Bikini

you will need for 1 glass:

4–5 ice cubes
juice ½ fresh lemon
1 teaspoon sugar or
  sugar syrup

1 part white rum
3 parts vodka
½ part milk

1 Put the ice cubes into a cocktail shaker.
3 Pour the lemon juice, sugar, rum, vodka and milk over the ice.
3 Shake until a frost forms; strain and pour into a lowball glass.

Vodka Alexander

you will need for 1 glass:

4–5 ice cubes	1 part thin cream
1 part crème de cacao	1 part vodka

1 Put the ice cubes into a cocktail shaker.
2 Pour the crème de cacao, cream and vodka over the ice.
3 Shake until a frost forms; strain and pour into a sour glass.

New Day

you will need for 1 glass:

4–5 ice cubes	3 parts vodka
1 part Calvados (apple brandy)	juice ½ fresh orange (or 2 tablespoons canned, unsweetened juice)
1 part apricot brandy	

1 Put the ice cubes into a cocktail shaker.
2 Pour the Calvados, apricot brandy, vodka and fruit juice over the ice.
3 Shake until a frost forms; strain and pour into a sour glass.

Here's how

you will need for 1 glass:

4–5 ice cubes	1 part vodka
juice 1 fresh lemon	½ teaspoon sugar or sugar syrup
1 part pale brandy	
1 egg white	

1 Put the ice cubes into a cocktail shaker.
2 Pour the lemon juice, brandy, vodka, sugar and egg white over the ice.
3 Shake until a frost forms; strain and pour into a sour glass.

Greybeard

you will need for 1 glass:

4–5 ice cubes	2 parts dry French vermouth
3 drops Angostura bitters	4 parts vodka
1 teaspoon cherry brandy	1 slice fresh lemon rind
1 part sweet Italian vermouth	

1 Put the ice cubes into a cocktail shaker.
2 Shake the bitters over the ice.
3 Pour in the cherry brandy, vermouths and vodka.
4 Shake lightly; strain and pour into a sour glass.
5 Twist the lemon rind over the mixture and drop it in.

Apollon

you will need for 1 glass:

4–5 ice cubes	juice 1 fresh lemon
3 drops orange bitters or Angostura bitters	1 part Cointreau
	3 parts vodka

1 Put the ice cubes into a cocktail shaker.
2 Shake the bitters and pour the fruit juice, Cointreau and vodka over the ice.
3 Shake lightly, strain and pour into a sour glass.

Elysium

you will need for 1 glass:

4–5 ice cubes	juice ½ fresh orange (or 2 tablespoons canned, unsweetened juice)
1 teaspoon bottled lime juice	1 part apricot brandy
	3 parts vodka

1 Put the ice cubes into a cocktail shaker.
2 Pour the lime juice, orange juice, brandy and vodka over the ice.
3 Shake until a frost forms; strain and pour into a sour glass.

Marguerite

you will need for 1 glass:

4–5 ice cubes	juice ½ fresh orange (or 2 tablespoons canned, unsweetened juice)
raspberry syrup or maraschino or grenadine	3 parts vodka
juice 1 fresh lemon	cracked ice

1 Put the ice cubes into a cocktail shaker.
2 Pour the syrup, fruit juices and vodka over the ice.
3 Shake the mixture until a frost forms.
4 Strain and pour into a lowball glass filled with cracked ice.

A Meadow

you will need for 1 glass:

4–5 ice cubes
crème de cacao
1 egg white
juice ½ fresh orange
(or 2 tablespoons
canned, unsweetened
juice)
2 parts vodka

1 Put the ice cubes into a cocktail shaker.
2 Pour the crème de cacao, orange juice, vodka and egg white over the ice.
3 Shake until a frost forms; strain and pour into a sour glass.

Forester

you will need for 1 glass:

4–5 ice cubes
juice ½ fresh grapefruit
(or 2½ tablespoons
canned, unsweetened
juice)
½ teaspoon grenadine
1 part dry French
vermouth
1 part sweet Italian
vermouth
3 parts vodka

1 Put the ice cubes into a cocktail shaker.
2 Pour the grapefruit juice, grenadine, vermouths and vodka over the ice.
3 Shake until a frost forms; strain and pour into a sour glass.

Maiden

you will need for 1 glass:

4–5 ice cubes
1 part Forbidden Fruit
1 part white crème de
menthe
2 parts vodka

1 Put the ice cubes into a cocktail shaker.
2 Pour the Forbidden Fruit, crème de menthe and vodka over the ice.
3 Shake until a frost forms; strain and pour into a chilled martini glass.

Commander

you will need for 1 glass:

4–5 ice cubes
juice ½ fresh grapefruit
(or 2½ tablespoons
canned, unsweetened
juice)
½ teaspoon Cointreau
1 part dry French
vermouth
1 part pale brandy
3 parts vodka

1 Put the ice cubes into a cocktail shaker.
2 Pour the grapefruit juice, Cointreau, vermouth, brandy and vodka over the ice.
3 Shake until a frost forms; strain and pour into a sour glass.

Pelican

you will need for 1 glass:

4–5 ice cubes
1 part sweet Italian
vermouth (white if
possible)
3 parts vodka
1 egg white

1 Whisk the egg white until stiff.
2 Put the ice cubes into a cocktail shaker.
3 Pour the vermouth, vodka, egg white over the ice.
4 Shake until a frost forms; strain and pour into a sour glass.

White Leopard

you will need for 1 glass:

4–5 ice cubes
juice ½ fresh lemon
juice ¼ fresh orange
(or 2 tablespoons
canned, unsweetened
juice)
1 part Grand Marnier
2 parts vodka

1 Put the ice cubes into a cocktail shaker.
2 Pour the fruit juices, Grand Marnier and vodka over the ice.
3 Shake until a frost forms; strain and pour into a sour glass.

Punches

For very large parties the simplest mixed drink to prepare and serve is a punch. Most punches improve by being prepared well ahead of time, and yet even these do not suffer when quickly replenished. And at punch parties it is usual for friends to help themselves which frees the host from bar tending.

By and large punches have a mild flavour, most pleasant, but also deceptive, for they are generally much stronger than most mixed drinks.

Cold Punches

Gin Punch

you will need for 12–14 persons:

ice	1 bottle gin
2 bottles dry white wine (Chablis, Blanc-de-Blanc or Hock)	½ pint cool green tea
	½ pint white rum
	2 fresh lemons, sliced

1 Put large chunks of ice into a punch bowl.
2 Pour the white wine, gin and tea over the ice.
3 Add the rum, and stir the mixture thoroughly.
4 Garnish with the sliced lemon; stir once more.

Orange Punch

you will need for 12–14 persons:

ice	2 tablespoons Curaçao
juice 6 fresh oranges (or 12 oz. canned, unsweetened)	1 bottle gin
	1 fresh orange, sliced
2 tablespoons sugar	1 siphon soda water

1 Put a large block of ice into a punch bowl.
2 Pour the orange juice, sugar, Curaçao and gin over the ice.
3 Stir the mixture thoroughly and garnish with orange slices.
4 Splash the soda water in at the last moment.

Valencia Punch

you will need for 12–14 persons:

ice	1 bottle dry white wine (Chablis, Hock or Spanish Chablis)
juice 6 fresh oranges (or 12 oz. canned, unsweetened juice)	
juice 3 fresh lemons	2 tablespoons white crème de menthe
fresh fruit	1 bottle gin

1 Put several large chunks of ice into a punch bowl.
2 Pour the fruit juices, wine, crème de menthe and gin over the ice.
3 Stir the mixture thoroughly.
4 Garnish with fresh fruit.

Blush Punch

you will need for 12–14 persons:

ice	2 bottles chilled rosé
juice 6 fresh lemons	1 bottle gin
2 tablespoons crème de Cassis or maraschino or grenadine	

1 Put several large chunks of ice into a punch bowl.
2 Pour the lemon juice, crème de Cassis, rosé and gin over the ice.
3 Stir thoroughly.

Dry Martini Punch

you will need for 12–14 persons:

ice	½ bottle extra dry sherry
rind 2 fresh lemons	2 bottles gin
½ bottle extra dry French vermouth	

1 Put several large chunks of ice into a punch bowl.
2 Cut the rind of each lemon into a continuous strip and put on the ice.
3 Pour in the vermouth, sherry and gin.
4 Stir thoroughly and let the mixture stand for a few minutes before serving.

Grapefruit Punch

you will need for 12–14 persons:

ice
juice 5 fresh grapefruit (or 15 tablespoons canned, unsweetened juice)
½ bottle sweet Italian vermouth
2 bottles gin
1 pint ice water
2 thinly sliced lemons

1 Put several large chunks of ice into a punch bowl.
2 Pour the grapefruit juice, vermouth and gin over the ice.
3 Stir thoroughly, then add the water.
4 Garnish with the sliced lemons.

Hawaiian Fruit Punch

you will need for 12–14 persons:

ice
1 pint pineapple juice
juice 3 fresh oranges (or 12 tablespoons canned, unsweetened juice)
juice 3 fresh lemons
½ bottle white rum
2 bottles gin
½ pint ice water
2 lemons
1 thinly sliced orange
wedges fresh pineapple

1 Put several large chunks of ice into a punch bowl.
2 Pour the fruit juices, rum and gin over the ice.
3 Stir the mixture thoroughly, and add the ice water.
4 Garnish with the fresh fruit and let stand for a few minutes.

Dubonnet Punch

you will need for 12–14 persons:

ice
juice 3 fresh lemons
2 bottles Dubonnet
2 bottles gin
1 pint ice water
2 thinly sliced lemons
6 sprigs young fresh mint (optional)

1 Put several large chunks of ice into a punch bowl.
2 Pour the lemon juice, Dubonnet and gin over the ice.
3 Stir thoroughly then add the ice water.
4 Garnish with the lemon slices and mint leaves if used.

Malakai Punch

you will need for 12–14 persons:

ice
8 oz. diced pineapple
juice 1 fresh lemon
2 dessertspoons grenadine
1 bottle dry white wine (Chablis, Blanc-de-Blanc or Hock)
½ bottle white rum
1 bottle gin
2 thinly sliced oranges

1 Put several large chunks of ice into a punch bowl.
2 Put the pineapple, lemon juice, grenadine, wine, rum and gin over the ice.
3 Stir the mixture thoroughly.
4 Garnish with the orange slices and let stand for while.

Fresh Fruit Punch

you will need for 12–14 persons:

3 pints fresh fruit, one variety or mixed (raspberries, strawberries, peaches, apricots, etc.)
½ pint sugar or sugar syrup
½ bottle white rum
ice
2 bottles dry white wine (Chablis, Blanc-de-Blanc or Hock)
1 bottle gin

This recipe demands time, for the fresh fruit must be marinated at least 6 hours before the punch can be prepared properly.

1 Wash the fruit, slice and put into a large bowl.
2 Pour the sugar and rum over the fruit and store it in the refrigerator for at least 6 hours.
3 Put several large chunks of ice into a punch bowl.
4 Put the marinated fruit over the ice, then add the wine and gin.
5 Stir the mixture thoroughly and let stand for 10 minutes before serving.

Picnic Punch

you will need for 12–14 persons:

ice
8 oz. diced pineapple
3 thinly sliced lemons
2 bottles dry white wine
   (Chablis, blanc-de-
   Blanc or Hock)
½ bottle white rum
1 bottle gin

1 Put several large chunks of ice into a punch bowl.

2 Scatter the fruit over the ice then pour in the wine, rum and gin.

3 Stir the mixture thoroughly and let it stand for a few minutes before serving.

Frosty Punch

you will need for 12–14 persons:

ice
3 tablespoons Pernod
1 bottle dry white wine
   (Chablis, Blanc-de-
   Blanc or Hock)
2 bottles gin
1 pint ice water

1 Put a large block of ice into a punch bowl.

2 Pour the Pernod, wine and gin over the ice.

3 Stir thoroughly; add the water and stir again.

4 Let stand for 15 minutes before serving.

Scotch Punch

you will need for 12–14 persons:

ice
½ pint cool green tea
1 pint brandy
2 bottles whisky
4 tablespoons sugar
   or sugar syrup
1 pint ice water
2 thinly sliced oranges

1 Put several large chunks of ice into a punch bowl.

2 Pour the tea, brandy, whisky and sugar over the ice.

3 Stir the mixture thoroughly; add the water and stir again.

4 Garnish with the orange slices and serve.

Manhattan Punch

you will need for 12–14 persons:

ice
1 bottle sweet Italian
   vermouth
¼ teaspoon Angostura
   bitters
2 bottles whisky
½ pint ice water
2 thinly sliced oranges
12 maraschino cherries
   (optional)

1 Put several large chunks of ice into a punch bowl.

2 Pour the vermouth, bitters and whisky over the ice.

3 Add the ice water and stir thoroughly.

4 Garnish with the fruit and serve.

Brigade Punch

you will need for 12–14 persons:

ice
1 pint cool green tea
2 tablespoons sugar or
   sugar syrup
½ bottle port
½ bottle brandy
1 bottle whisky
rind 1 fresh lemon

1 Put several large chunks of ice into a punch bowl.

2 Pour the tea, sugar, port, brandy and whisky over the ice.

3 Stir the mixture thoroughly, garnish with the fresh lemon rind and serve.

Artillery Punch

you will need for 12–14 persons:

ice
juice 3 fresh lemons
2 tablespoons sugar or
   sugar syrup
1 tablespoon
   Angostura bitters
½ bottle medium dry
   sherry
½ bottle claret
½ bottle brandy
1 bottle whisky

1 Put several large chunks of ice into a punch bowl.

2 Pour the lemon juice, sugar, bitters, wines, brandy and whisky over the ice.

3 Stir the mixture thoroughly and let stand a few minutes and serve.

Festoon Punch

you will need for 12–14 persons:

1 large block ice
juice 3 fresh lemons
2 pints cool tea
1 bottle whisky
½ pint dark rum
½ pint Curaçao
½ bottle dry sherry
1 bottle hock
rind 1 fresh lemon

1 Put the ice into a punch bowl.

2 Pour the lemon juice, tea, whisky, rum, Curaçao, sherry and hock over the ice.

3 Stir the mixture thoroughly.

4 Garnish with the lemon rind.

5 Let stand a few minutes and serve.

Sour Punch

you will need for 12–14 persons:

ice
juice 6 fresh oranges
  (or ¾ pint canned,
  unsweetened juice)
Juice 2 fresh lemons
2 tablespoons sugar or
  sugar syrup

1 bottle whisky
1 siphon soda water
1 orange
1 thinly sliced lemon

1 Put several large chunks of ice into a punch bowl.
2 Pour the fruit juices, sugar, and whisky over the ice.
3 Stir the mixture thoroughly and garnish with the fresh fruit.
4 Add the soda water at the last minute.

Brandy Punch

you will need for 12–14 persons:

1 large block ice
juice 2 fresh oranges
  (or 8 tablespoons
  canned, unsweetened
  juice)
juice 6 fresh lemons

2 tablespoons sugar or
  sugar syrup
½ pint Curaçao
1 bottle brandy
1 tablespoon grenadine
soda water

1 Put the ice into a punch bowl.
2 Pour the fruit juices, sugar, Curaçao, brandy and grenadine over the ice.
3 Stir the mixture thoroughly and at the last minute add the soda water.

Chatham Punch

you will need for 12–14 persons:

ice
juice 6 fresh oranges
  (or ¾ pint canned,
  unsweetened juice)
juice 6 fresh lemons
3 tablespoons sugar or
  sugar syrup

1 pint cool green tea
½ pint whisky
½ pint dark rum
1 bottle hock
1 bottle brandy

1 Put several large chunks of ice into a punch bowl.
2 Pour the fruit juices, sugar, tea, whisky, rum, hock and brandy over the ice.
3 Stir the mixture thoroughly and let stand a few minutes before serving.

Jubel Early Punch

you will need for 12–14 persons:

ice
juice 12 fresh lemons
3 tablespoons sugar
  or sugar syrup

1 pint dark rum
1 bottle Moselle
1 bottle brandy

1 Put several large chunks of ice into a punch bowl.
2 Pour the lemon juice, sugar, rum, Moselle and brandy over the ice.
3 Stir the mixture thoroughly and let stand a few minutes before serving.

Black Velvet Punch

you will need for 12–14 persons:

ice
juice 6 fresh lemons
3 tablespoons sugar
  or sugar syrup
2 pints stout

1 tablespoon Angostura
  bitters
1 orange
1 thinly sliced lemon
1 bottle Champagne

1 Put several large chunks of ice into a punch bowl.
2 Pour the lemon juice, sugar, stout and bitters over the ice.
3 Stir the mixture thoroughly.
4 Garnish with the fresh fruit.
5 At the last minute pour in the Champagne and serve.

Fisherman's Punch

you will need for 12–14 persons:

ice	½ bottle brandy
juice 4 fresh lemons	4 tablespoons peach
3 tablespoons sugar	brandy
or sugar syrup	1 bottle whisky
½ bottle dark rum	

1 Put several large chunks of ice into a punch bowl.
2 Pour the lemon juice, sugar, rum, brandies and whisky over the ice.
3 Stir the mixture thoroughly and serve.

Boston Fish House Punch

you will need for 12–14 persons:

ice	1 bottle brandy
juice 6 fresh lemons	4 tablespoons peach
4 tablespoons sugar	brandy
or sugar syrup	2 bottles Champagne
1 bottle dark rum	

1 Put several large chunks of ice into a large punch bowl.
2 Pour the lemon juice, sugar, rum and brandies over the ice.
3 Stir the mixture thoroughly and at the last minute pour in the Champagne.

Southern Punch

you will need for 12–14 persons:

ice	2 tablespoons
juice 6 fresh lemons	maraschino
4 tablespoons sugar	or grenadine
or sugar syrup	1 orange
2 bottles claret	1 lemon
½ pint dry sherry	½ thinly sliced cucumber
1 pint brandy	1 bottle dry ginger ale
1 bottle dark rum	1 siphon soda water

1 Put several large chunks of ice into a punch bowl.
2 Pour the lemon juice, sugar, claret, sherry, brandy, rum and maraschino over the ice.
3 Stir the mixture thoroughly and garnish with the sliced fruit and cucumber.
4 At the last minute pour in the dry ginger ale and add the soda water.

Prinny Punch

you will need for 12–14 persons:

rind of 2 fresh lemons	juice 6 fresh oranges
1 pint strong cold	(or ¾ pint canned,
Indian tea	unsweetened juice)
ice	juice 6 fresh lemons
2 tablespoons sugar or	1 bottle brandy
sugar syrup	½ bottle dark rum
	1 bottle Champagne

1 Put the lemon rind into the tea and stir.
2 Put several large chunks of ice into a punch bowl.
3 Pour the lemon-flavoured tea, sugar, fruit juices, brandy and rum over the ice.
4 Stir the mixture thoroughly and just before serving pour in the Champagne.

West Indian Punch

you will need for 12–14 persons:

juice 4 fresh grapefruit	2 teaspoons
(or 1 pint canned,	Angostura bitters
unsweetened juice)	ice
juice 2 fresh oranges	½ bottle brandy
(or 8 tablespoons	4 tablespoons
canned, unsweetened	Bénédictine
juice)	1 bottle dark rum
2 tablespoons sugar	grated nutmeg
or sugar syrup	rind 1 fresh lemon

1 Put the fruit juices, sugar and bitters into a punch bowl.
2 Stir the mixture thoroughly, then add several large chunks of ice.
3 Pour the brandy, Bénédictine and rum over the ice.
4 Stir thoroughly and lavishly sprinkle the nutmeg into the drink.
5 Garnish with the lemon rind and serve.

Claret Punch

you will need for 12–14 persons:

ice	1 teaspoon Angostura
juice 3 fresh oranges	bitters
(or 12 tablespoons	8 oz. pineapple chunks
canned, unsweetened	½ bottle brandy
juice)	2 bottles claret
juice 3 fresh lemons	½ siphon soda water
2 tablespoons sugar	
or sugar syrup	

1 Fill a punch bowl with large chunks of ice.
2 Pour in the fruit juices, sugar, bitters, pineapple chunks, brandy and claret.
3 Stir the mixture thoroughly and just before serving add the soda water.

White Wine Punch

you will need for 12–14 persons:

Ice
½ pint extra dry sherry
4 tablespoons Pernod
4 tablespoons brandy
2 bottles dry white wine (Blanc-de-Blanc, Chablis or Hock)
rind 1 fresh lemon
soda water

1 Put several large chunks of ice into a punch bowl.
2 Pour the sherry, Pernod, brandy and wine over the ice.
3 Stir the mixture thoroughly.
4 Garnish with the fresh fruit.
5 At the last minute add the soda and serve.

Sparkling Punch

you will need for 12–14 persons:

ice
1 tablespoon sugar or sugar syrup
½ bottle brandy
1 bottle claret
½ siphon soda water
fresh strawberries or raspberries
2 bottles Champagne

1 Put several large chunks of ice into a punch bowl.
2 Pour the sugar, brandy and claret over the ice.
3 Stir the mixture well and add the soda water.
4 Garnish with the fresh fruit and just before serving pour in the Champagne.

Golden Punch

you will need for 12–14 persons:

ice
3 tablespoons yellow Chartreuse
1 tablespoon maraschino or grenadine
½ pint brandy
1 split soda
2 thinly sliced fresh oranges
3 bottles Champagne

1 Put several large chunks of ice into a punch bowl.
2 Pour the Chartreuse, maraschino and brandy over the ice.
3 Stir the mixture well and add the split of soda.
4 Garnish with the orange slices and just before serving pour in the chilled Champagne.

Champagne Punch

you will need for 12–14 persons:

2 tablespoons sugar or sugar syrup
1 teaspoon Angostura bitters
3 thinly sliced fresh oranges
3 thinly sliced fresh lemons
1 split soda water
Ice
3 bottles Champagne

1 Put the sugar, bitters and fruit juices into a punch bowl.
2 Stir the mixture thoroughly, add the soda water.
3 Put in several large chunks of ice and stir again.
4 At the last minute pour in the chilled Champagne and serve.

Dragoon Punch

you will need for 12–14 persons:

ice
½ pint dry sherry
½ pint brandy
3 half bottles stout
3 half bottles lager
2 bottles Champagne
2 thinly sliced lemons

1 Put several large chunks of ice into a punch bowl.
2 Pour the sherry, brandy, stout and lager over the ice.
3 Stir the mixture thoroughly, garnish with lemons and at the last minute pour in the Champagne.

Hot Punches

It is best to use a porcelain pan in preparing these, or if you have one, a chafing dish. This latter will keep the punch warm at the table.

Bishop's Punch

you will need for 12–14 persons:

12 cloves	3 tablespoons sugar or
2 fresh oranges	sugar syrup
3 drops Angostura	2 bottles port
bitters	grated nutmeg

1 Stick the cloves into each of the oranges.
2 Bake the oranges until the rind becomes brown.
3 Cut the oranges into quarters and put them into a porcelain pan.
4 Shake the bitters over the oranges.
5 Add the sugar and port.
6 Heat the mixture and let it simmer for about 15 minutes.
7 Spoon the mixture into stem glasses and sprinkle the top with grated nutmeg.

Oxford Punch

you will need for 20 persons:

juice and rind 6 fresh	10 oz. calf's foot jelly
lemons	½ bottle dark rum
juice and rind 4 fresh	1 bottle brandy
oranges (or ½ pint	½ bottle dry sherry
canned, unsweetened	4 tablespoons Curaçao
juice)	1 tablespoon Angostura
4 pints boiling water	bitters

1 Pour the fruit juices and the rinds into the boiling water.
2 Add the calf's foot jelly and let the mixture simmer for about 30 minutes.
3 Pour the mixture into a warmed bowl; add the rum, brandy, sherry, Curaçao and bitters.
4 Spoon into punch cups.

Hot Rum Punch

you will need for 12–14 persons:

juice 6 fresh lemons	½ bottle brandy
2 tablespoons sugar or	1 bottle dark rum
sugar syrup	½ bottle dry sherry
1 teaspoon ground	2 pints boiling water
ginger	grated nutmeg

1 Pour the lemon juice, sugar and ground ginger into a warmed bowl.
2 Mix well, then add the brandy, rum, sherry and hot water.
3 Stir well and spoon the mixture into punch cups.
4 Grate a little nutmeg into each cup.

Warm Air Flip

you will need for 4 persons:

4 fresh eggs	nutmeg
4 tablespoons sugar or	2 pints ale
sugar syrup	

1 Separate the egg yolks from the whites.
2 Whip the whites of 2 eggs until frothy, then add the sugar and nutmeg.
3 Continue whipping then add the 4 egg yolks.
4 Pour the ale into a pan and heat until it froths.
5 Add the beaten egg mixture, gradually stirring the boiling ale all the time.
6 When this comes to a frothy lather, spoon the mixture into mugs and serve.

Hot Brandy Punch

you will need for 12–14 persons:

rind 2 fresh lemons	6 tablespoons sugar
cinnamon	or sugar syrup
nutmeg	½ pint boiling water
mace	juice 2 fresh lemons
cloves	1 bottle brandy

1 Put the lemon rind, spices and sugar into the boiling water, and let simmer for 10 minutes.
2 Strain and pour the mixture into a warmed punch bowl.
3 Add the lemon juice and brandy.
4 Set the mixture alight and spoon into punch cups.

Café Grog

you will need for 6–8 persons:

1 pint fresh hot coffee	6 tablespoons brandy
2 tablespoons sugar or	1 bottle dark rum
sugar syrup	1 thinly sliced lemon

1 Pour the coffee, nearly, but not boiling, into a warmed punch bowl.
2 Add the sugar, brandy and rum: stir the mixture.
3 Garnish with the sliced lemon and spoon into punch cups.

Glow Cup
you will need for 8–10 persons:

2 bottles red, unfortified wine (Burgundy, Claret Tinto)	cloves
	rind 1 fresh lemon
	1 stick cinnamon
6 tablespoons sugar or sugar syrup	1 thinly sliced orange

1 Put the wine, sugar, cloves, lemon rind, cinnamon into a pan and bring it to the boil.
2 Let this simmer for 10 minutes.
3 Spoon this into punch cups and into each put 1 slice of orange.

Christmas Rum Punch
you will need for 18 persons:

60 cloves	2 bottles cider
fresh oranges	cinnamon
½ bottle brandy	ground nutmeg
1 bottle dark rum	
4 tablespoons sugar or sugar syrup	

1 Stick about 10 cloves into each orange and bake these until the rind becomes brown.
2 Put the baked oranges into a warmed punch bowl and add the brandy, rum and sugar.
3 Stir the mixture thoroughly, and set it alight.
4 Slowly add the cider, putting out the flame.
5 Sprinkle the top with cinnamon and nutmeg.
6 Stir and spoon into punch cups.

Hot Buttered Rum
you will need for 16 persons:

6 tablespoons soft brown sugar	1 bottle dark rum
½ pint boiling water	pat butter
2 bottles cider	ground cinnamon

1 Put the sugar and boiling water into a porcelain pan.
2 Heat, stirring constantly, and slowly add the cider.
3 When this mixture comes to the boil, add the rum and the butter.
4 Spoon the mixture into mugs and sprinkle the top with cinnamon.

Hot Toddy
you will need for 10–12 persons:

2 thinly sliced fresh lemons	4 tablespoons sugar
6 cloves	1 stick cinnamon
1 bottle whisky	4 pints boiling water

1 Stud the lemon slices with three cloves each.
2 Pour the whisky, sugar and cinnamon into a pan.
3 When this nearly comes to the boil add the water.
4 Put the spiced lemon slices into mugs and pour the mixture over them.

Whisky Punch
you will need for 8–10 persons:

juice and rind 2 fresh lemons	12 cloves
6 tablespoons sugar	1 bottle whisky
cinnamon	1 pint boiling water

1 Pour the lemon juice and sugar into a warmed punch bowl.
2 Add the cut up rinds, cinnamon and cloves.
3 Mix thoroughly; add the whisky and boiling water.
4 Stir and spoon into punch cups.

Mint and Burgundy Punch

you will need for 14–16 persons:

5 sprigs fresh mint	1 stick cinnamon
rind 1 fresh lemon	8 cloves
6 tablespoons sugar	1 bottle Burgundy or
or sugar syrup	vino Tinto
1 tablespoon grenadine	1 pint boiling water

1 Put the mint, lemon juice, sugar and grenadine into a warmed punch bowl.
2 Mix thoroughly; add the spices and Burgundy.
3 Stir the mixture slowly adding the boiling water.
4 Spoon into punch cups.

Sack Posset

you will need for 10–12 persons:

2 pints milk	1 tablespoon sugar
1 bottle medium dry	or sugar syrup
sherry	nutmeg
1 pint ale	

1 Warm the milk in a saucepan.
2 At the same time in another saucepan heat the sherry and ale and when it comes to the boil add the sugar.
3 Slowly transfer the mixture into the warming milk, stirring all the time.
4 Lower the flame and let simmer for 10 minutes.
5 Pour into mugs, sprinkle with nutmeg and serve.

Hot Tea Punch

you will need for 12–14 persons:

4 pints hot tea	2 tablespoons sugar
1 bottle dark rum	1 lemon
½ bottle brandy	2 thinly sliced oranges

1 Pour the hot tea into a warmed punch bowl.
2 Add the rum, brandy and sugar.
3 Stir the mixture well.
4 Garnish with the fresh fruit and serve.

Ski Punch

you will need for 12–14 persons:

1 pint tea	sugar
juice 3 fresh lemons	2 tablespoons Curaçao
juice 6 fresh oranges	1 bottle dark rum
(or ¾ pint canned,	
unsweetened juice)	

1 Heat the tea, fruit juices and sugar until the mixture comes to the boil.
2 Pour the Curaçao and rum into a warmed punch bowl and add the boiling tea mixture.
3 Stir thoroughly; spoon and serve in mugs.

Negus Cup

you will need for 10–12 persons:

1 bottle port	juice and rind 1 lemon
1 tablespoon sugar or	1 teaspoon nutmeg
sugar syrup	2 pints boiling water

1 Pour the port, lemon juice and sugar into a warmed punch bowl.
2 Add the cut up lemon rind and the grated nutmeg.
3 At the last moment pour in the boiling water.
4 Stir and spoon into punch cups.

Tom and Jerry

you will need for 12–14 persons:

6 eggs	1 bottle brandy
3 tablespoons sugar	1 pint boiling water or
or sugar syrup	milk
½ bottle rum	grated nutmeg

1 Separate the eggs.
2 Whip the whites until stiff.
3 Beat the yolks until smooth.
4 Fold the beaten egg yolks into the stiff egg whites.
5 Add sugar, stir gently and pour mixture into a warmed punch bowl.
6 Very slowly add the rum and brandy, stirring constantly to avoid curdling.
7 Pour in the boiling milk or water and sprinkle with nutmeg.
8 Stir gently and serve in mugs.

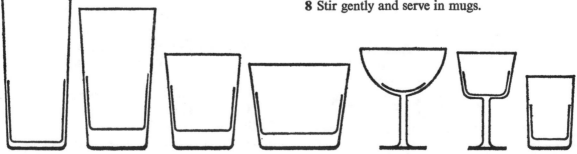

Boilermaker Punch

you will need for 14–16 persons:

juice and rind 1 fresh lemon
2 tablespoons sugar or sugar syrup
2 pints boiling water
1 pint ale
½ bottle brandy
1 bottle whisky

1 Put the lemon juice, sugar and water into a saucepan and heat until the mixture comes to the boil.
2 At the same time in another saucepan heat the ale until it comes to a boil.
3 Pour these mixtures into a warmed punch bowl.
4 Add the sliced lemon rind, brandy and whisky.
5 Stir gently and serve in mugs.

Northern Punch

you will need for 10–12 persons:

4 eggs
1 tablespoon sugar or sugar syrup
¼ bottle brandy
1 bottle light rum
1 tablespoon grated nutmeg
1 pint boiling water

1 Separate the eggs.
2 Beat the yolks until smooth.
3 Whip the whites until stiff.
4 Fold the egg yolks into the stiff egg white.
5 Add the sugar and mix gently.
6 Pour the mixture in a warmed punch bowl.
7 Add the brandy and rum.
8 Sprinkle the nutmeg over and stir gently.
9 Add the boiling water, stir and serve in mugs.

One A.M. Punch

you will need for 14 persons:

sliced rind 2 fresh lemons
2 tablespoons sugar or sugar syrup
2 pints milk
1 cup tea
1 bottle Calvados (apple brandy)
grated nutmeg

1 Combine the sliced lemon rind, sugar and milk in a pan and bring to the boil.
2 Add the tea and Calvados and let simmer for 10 minutes.
3 Spoon into mugs.
4 Sprinkle the top with grated nutmeg and serve.

Mulled Wine

you will need for 8–10 persons:

1 bottle and 2 glasses red wine
1 tablespoon sugar
1 teaspoon nutmeg
4 egg yolks

1 Pour the bottle of wine into a pan, sweetened with the sugar.
2 Add the grated nutmeg and bring to the boil.
3 Whip the egg yolks with 2 glasses of red wine.
4 As the wine comes to the boil, slowly add the egg yolk mixture stirring all the time.
5 When the mixture thickens spoon it into mugs and serve.

Egg Nogs

Egg nogs are mostly served at Christmas and the New Year. They are very rich but delicious, served warm or cold. It is wiser to make small amounts each time, for one or two glasses go a long way.

Basic Egg Nog

you will need for 10–12 persons:

6 fresh eggs
6 tablespoons sugar
1 pint milk
½ bottle whisky
¼ pint dark rum
1 pint thick cream
3 tablespoons peach brandy
grated nutmeg

1 Separate the eggs, putting the whites into a large bowl.
2 Beat the egg yolks until smooth adding sugar and ½ pint milk at the same time.
3 Pour this mixture into a punch bowl.
4 Add the whisky, mixing well, then add rum.
5 Set this aside and whip the egg whites until they are stiff.
6 Add the remaining milk, cream and peach brandy to the punch bowl.
7 Stir this together and fold in the egg white.
8 Sprinkle the grated nutmeg on top and serve.

Sweet Egg Nog

you will need for 12–14 persons:

6 eggs
8 tablespoons sugar
½ bottle whisky
½ pint rum
½ pint brandy
2 pints milk
2 pints thick cream
½ teaspoon ground cloves
½ teaspoon ground nutmeg

1 Separate the eggs, putting the whites into a mixing bowl and the yolks into the punch bowl.
2 Beat the egg yolks until smooth, adding 4 tablespoons sugar at the same time.
3 Still stirring, gradually add the whisky, rum and brandy.
4 Set this mixture aside and whip the egg whites until stiff adding the remaining sugar.
5 Then stir the milk and cream into the mixture in the punch bowl.
6 Fold in stiff egg whites.
7 Sprinkle with the cloves and nutmegs and serve.

Baltimore Egg Nog

you will need for 14–16 persons:

6 eggs
6 tablespoons sugar
1 pint Madeira
½ bottle dark rum
½ bottle brandy
2 pints milk
2 pints thick cream
1 teaspoon grated nutmeg

1 Separate the eggs, putting the whites into a mixing bowl and the yolks into the punch bowl.
2 Beat the egg yolks until smooth, gradually adding the sugar.
3 Still stirring, slowly add the Madeira, rum and brandy.
4 Whip the egg whites until very stiff.
5 Pour the milk and cream into the punch bowl and whip the mixture vigorously.
6 Fold in the egg whites.
7 Sprinkle the top with nutmeg and serve.

Frozen Egg Nog

you will need for 8–10 persons:

2 pints thick cream
6 egg yolks
8 tablespoons sugar
½ bottle rum
½ bottle brandy
1 teaspoon grated nutmeg

1 Whip the cream until stiff and store in the refrigerator.
2 Beat the egg yolks until smooth, adding the sugar at the same time.
3 Combine with the whipped cream.
4 Store in the refrigerator until firm.
5 Add the rum and brandy to the frozen mixture.
6 Sprinkle with nutmeg and serve.

Lion Egg Nog

you will need for 8–10 persons:

12 eggs
12 teaspoons sugar
½ bottle whisky
½ bottle dark rum
1 pint thick cream
2 pints milk
1 teaspoon grated nutmeg

1 Separate the eggs, putting the whites into a mixing bowl and the yolks into the punch bowl.
2 Beat the yolks until smooth, adding the sugar at the same time.
3 Gradually add the whisky and rum stirring all the time.
4 Whip the cream until stiff, then fold into the mixture in the punch bowl.
5 Add the milk.
6 Stir together.
7 Whip the egg whites until stiff.
8 Combine the egg whites with the mixture.
9 Stir gently; sprinkle with nutmeg and serve.

Wine Cocktails

Champagne Cocktail

you will need for 1 glass:

1 lump cube sugar
2 drops Angostura
  bitters
1 tablespoon brandy
4 parts iced Champagne
1 slice fresh lemon
  (optional)

1 Put the lump of sugar into the base of a Champagne glass.
2 Shake the bitters on to the sugar.
3 Add the brandy.
4 Pour in the iced Champagne.
5 Garnish with lemon and serve.

Walsh's Champagne Cocktail

you will need for 1 glass:

chopped ice
1 cube sugar
Iced Champagne
1 sprig fresh mint
1 slice fresh lemon
  rind
1 maraschino cherry
  (optional)

1 Fill a highball glass with chopped ice.
2 Put the lump of sugar on top of the ice.
3 Fill the glass with Champagne.
4 Garnish with the mint, lemon and cherry.

Sherry Cocktail

you will need for 1 glass:

4–5 ice cubes
1 part dry French
  vermouth
3 parts extra dry sherry
1 slice fresh lemon
  rind

1 Put the ice cubes into a glass jug.
2 Pour the vermouth and sherry over the ice.
3 Stir vigorously; strain and pour into a chilled martini glass.
4 Twist the lemon rind over the drink and drop it in.

Port Cocktail

you will need for 1 glass:

4–5 ice cubes
2 drops Angostura
  bitters
1 teaspoon Curaçao
3 parts port

1 Put the ice cubes into a glass jug.
2 Put the bitters, Curaçao and port over the ice.
3 Stir vigorously; strain and pour into a chilled martini glass.

Coffee Wine Cocktail

you will need for 1 glass:

4–5 ice cubes
1 egg yolk
1 teaspoon sugar or
  sugar syrup
1 part brandy
3 parts port
grated nutmeg

1 Put the ice cubes into a cocktail shaker.
2 Pour the egg yolk, sugar, brandy and port over the ice.
3 Shake until a frost forms; strain and pour into a sour glass.
4 Sprinkle grated nutmeg over the mixture and serve.

Vin Blanc Cassis (Kir)

you will need for 1 glass:

2–3 ice cubes
3 teaspoons crème de
  Cassis
4 parts dry white wine
  (Blanc-de-Blanc,
  Chablis, or Hock)

1 Put the ice cubes into a lowball glass.
2 Pour the Cassis and wine over the ice.
3 Stir gently and serve.

Vin Blanc Vermouth

you will need for 1 glass:

2–3 ice cubes
1 part dry French
  vermouth
3 parts dry white wine
  (Blanc-de-Blanc,
  Chablis, or Hock)
1 slice fresh lemon rind

1 Put the ice cubes into a lowball glass.
2 Pour the vermouth and wine over the ice.
3 Stir gently.
4 Garnish with the lemon rind and serve.

Wine Cooler

you will need for 1 glass:

3 ice cubes
red or white wine
soda water
1 slice fresh lemon rind

1 Put the ice cubes into a lowball glass.
2 Pour the wine over the ice and top with soda water.
3 Garnish with the lemon rind and serve.

Tonic Cooler

you will need for 1 glass:

3 ice cubes
white wine
tonic water

1 slice fresh lemon
rind

1 Put the ice cubes into a lowball glass.
2 Pour the wine over the ice.
3 Add the tonic water.
4 Garnish with the lemon rind and serve.

Sherry Old-Fashioned

you will need for 1 glass:

1 cube sugar
2 drops Angostura
  bitters
2–3 ice cubes

3 parts medium dry
  sherry
1 slice fresh lemon rind
1 maraschino cherry
  (optional)

1 Put the lump of sugar into the base of an old-fashioned glass.
2 Shake the bitters over the sugar; swirl round the sides of the glass.
3 Put the ice cubes into the glass.
4 Pour the sherry over the ice; stir gently.
5 Garnish with the lemon rind and cherry and serve.

American Beauty

you will need for 1 glass:

3 ice cubes
1 part Muscatel

4 parts Champagne
  (thoroughly chilled)
1 fresh peeled grape

1 Put the ice cubes into a lowball glass.
2 Pour the wines over the ice.
3 Garnish with the grape and serve.

Arise My Love

you will need for 1 glass:

1 teaspoon white
  crème de menthe

4 parts Champagne
  (thoroughly chilled)

1 Pour the crème de menthe into a Champagne glass and swirl it round the glass.
2 Pour in the Champagne and serve.

Death in the Afternoon

you will need for 1 glass:

1 part Pernod

4 parts Champagne
  (thoroughly chilled)

1 Put the Pernod into a Champagne glass, and swirl it round.
2 Slowly pour in the iced Champagne allowing the drink to become cloudy.
3 Serve.

Merry Widow

you will need for 1 glass:

3–4 ice cubes
1 part dry French
  vermouth

3 parts Dubonnet

1 Put the ice cubes into a glass jug.
2 Pour the vermouth and Dubonnet over the ice.
3 Stir vigorously; strain and pour into a chilled martini glass.

Sensation

you will need for 1 glass:

4–5 ice cubes
1 part brandy

3 parts port
1 slice fresh lemon rind

1 Put the ice cubes into a glass jug.
2 Pour the brandy and port over the ice.
3 Stir vigorously; strain and pour into a chilled martini glass.
4 Garnish with the lemon rind and serve.

Sherry Cobbler

you will need for 1 glass:

4–5 ice cubes
1 teaspoon sugar or
  sugar syrup

1 part Curaçao
3 parts dry sherry
  port

1 Put four or five ice cubes into a glass jug.
2 Pour the sugar, Curaçao and sherry over the ice.
3 Stir vigorously; pour without straining into a lowball glass.
4 Top with port and serve.

Champagne Cobbler

you will need for 1 glass:

4–5 ice cubes
1 teaspoon sugar or
  sugar syrup

1 part crème de cacao
juice 1 fresh lemon
3 parts Champagne

1 Put the ice cubes into a glass jug.
2 Pour the sugar, crème de cacao and lemon juice over the ice.
3 Stir vigorously and pour without straining into a lowball glass.
4 Top with Champagne.

Port Cobbler

you will need for 1 glass:

4–5 ice cubes
1 part brandy

juice 1 fresh lemon
3 parts white port

1 Put the ice cubes into a glass jug.
2 Pour the brandy, lemon juice and port over the ice.
3 Stir vigorously and pour without straining into a lowball glass.

Red Lady

you will need for 1 glass:

3 ice cubes   1 part vodka
3 parts red wine
  (Burgundy, Claret or
  vino Tinto)

1 Put the ice cubes into a glass jug.
2 Pour the wine and vodka over the ice.
3 Stir vigorously; strain and pour into a chilled martini glass.

La Dame Blanche

you will need for 1 glass:

4–5 ice cubes   1 part vodka
3 parts dry white wine
  (Chablis, Hock or
  Muscadet)

1 Put the ice cubes into a glass jug.
2 Pour the wine and vodka over the ice.
3 Stir vigorously; strain and pour into a chilled martini glass.

Dubonnet and Lime

you will need for 1 glass:

4–5 ice cubes   3 parts Dubonnet
1 part bottled lime juice

1 Put the ice cubes into a glass jug.
2 Pour the lime juice and Dubonnet over the ice.
3 Stir vigorously; strain and pour into a chilled martini glass.

Red Ensign

you will need for 1 glass:

4–5 ice cubes   1 part vodka
3 parts port   1 slice fresh lemon rind

1 Put the ice cubes into a glass jug.
2 Pour the port and vodka over the ice.

3 Stir vigorously; strain and pour into a chilled martini glass.
4 Twist the lemon rind over the drink and drop it in.

Royal Plush

you will need for 1 glass:

3 ice cubes   1 part Champagne
1 part red Burgundy

1 Put the ice cubes into a highball glass.
2 Pour the wines over the ice.
3 Stir gently and serve.

American Glory

you will need for 1 glass:

3 ice cubes   2 part Champagne
juice ½ fresh orange   1 part soda water
  (or 2 tablespoons
  canned, unsweetened
  juice)

1 Put the ice cubes into a highball glass.
2 Pour the orange juice and Champagne over the ice.
3 Add the soda water.
4 Stir gently and serve.

San Francisco Dubonnet

you will need for 1 glass:

3 ice cubes   1 part extra dry sherry
2 drops orange bitters   1 slice fresh lemon
  or Angostura   rind
  bitters   1 maraschino cherry
2 part Dubonnet

1 Put the ice cubes into a glass jug.
2 Shake the bitters over the ice.
3 Add the Dubonnet and sherry.
4 Stir vigorously; strain and pour into a chilled martini glass.
5 Twist the lemon rind over the mixture, drop it in, add the cherry and serve.

London Dubonnet

you will need for 1 glass:

4–5 ice cubes
3 drops orange bitters
3 drops Angostura
  bitters
2 parts Dubonnet

1 part dry French
  vermouth
1 part extra dry sherry
1 slice fresh orange rind

1 Put the ice cubes into a glass jug.
2 Shake the bitters and pour the Dubonnet, vermouth and sherry over the ice.
3 Stir vigorously; strain and put into a chilled martini glass.
4 Twist the orange rind over the drink and drop it in.

Brazil

you will need for 1 glass:

4–5 ice cubes
3 drops orange bitters
½ teaspoon sugar or
  sugar syrup
1 teaspoon Pernod

1 part dry French
  vermouth
3 parts medium dry
  sherry

1 Put the ice cubes into a glass jug.
2 Shake the bitters over the ice.
3 Add the sugar, Pernod, vermouth and sherry.
4 Stir vigorously; strain and pour into a chilled martini glass.

Quartier Latin

you will need for 1 glass:

4–5 ice cubes
1 part Cointreau

1 part Amer Picon
3 parts Dubonnet

1 Put the ice cubes into a glass jug.
2 Pour the Cointreau, Amer Picon, Dubonnet over the ice.
3 Stir vigorously; strain and pour into a chilled martini glass.

Wine Collins

you will need for 1 glass:

4–5 ice cubes
juice fresh lemons
1 tablespoon sugar or
  sugar syrup

3 parts dry white wine
  (Chablis, Hock or
  Muscadet)
soda water

1 Put the ice cubes into a glass jug.
2 Pour the lemon juice, sugar and wine over the ice.
3 Stir vigorously; pour, without straining, into a collins glass.
4 Top with soda water and serve.

Bright Morning

you will need for 1 glass:

4–5 ice cubes
juice 1 fresh orange
  (or 4 tablespoons
  canned, unsweetened
  juice)

1 tablespoon grenadine
4 parts dry white wine
  (Chablis, Hock or
  Muscadet)
soda water

1 Put the ice cubes into a glass jug.
2 Pour the orange juice, grenadine and wine over the ice.
3 Stir vigorously and pour, without straining, into a collins glass.
4 Top with soda water, stir gently and serve.

Paris Mist

you will need for 1 glass:

3 ice cubes
5 drops Pernod

3 parts dry white wine
  (Blanc-de-Blanc,
  Chablis, Muscadet)

1 Put the ice cubes into a lowball glass.
2 Pour the Pernod over the ice and add the wine.
3 Stir gently and serve.

Guadaloupe

you will need for 1 glass:

4–5 ice cubes
juice 1 fresh lemon
3 drops Angostura
  bitters

3 parts dry white wine
  (Blanc-de-Blanc,
  Chablis, Muscadet)

1 Put the ice cubes into a glass jug.
2 Shake the bitters, the fruit juice and wine over the ice.
3 Stir vigorously; strain and pour into a chilled martini glass.

San Remo

you will need for 1 glass:

4–5 ice cubes
1 part sweet Italian
  vermouth

3 parts dry white wine
  (Chablis, white
  Chianti, or Suave)
1 slice fresh lemon rind

1 Put the ice cubes into a glass jug.
2 Pour the vermouth and wine over the ice.
3 Stir vigorously; strain and pour into a chilled martini glass.
4 Twist the lemon rind over the mixture and drop it in.

Pagera

you will need for 1 glass:

3–4 ice cubes
1 part extra dry sherry
3 parts dry white
  Spanish wine
  (Spanish Chablis,
  Vino Secco)

1 slice fresh lemon rind

1 Put the ice cubes into a glass jug.
2 Pour the sherry and wine over the ice.
3 Stir vigorously; strain and pour into a chilled martini glass.
4 Twist the lemon rind over the drink and drop it in.

Baton Blanc

you will need for 1 glass:

4–5 ice cubes
3 drops orange or
  Angostura bitters
1 part dry French
  vermouth

3 parts dry white wine
  (Chablis, Hock or
  Muscadet)

1 Put the ice cubes into a glass jug.
2 Shake the bitters over the ice and add the vermouth and wine.
3 Stir vigorously; strain and pour into a chilled martini glass.

Petit Piton

you will need for 1 glass:

4–5 ice cubes
Juice 1 fresh orange
  (or 4 tablespoons
  canned, unsweetened
  juice)
Juice 1 fresh lime or
  lemon

3 drops Angostura
  bitters
3 parts dry white wine
  (Blanc-de-Blanc,
  Chablis or Muscadet)

1 Put the ice cubes into a glass jug.
2 Pour the fruit juices, bitters and the wine over the ice.
3 Stir vigorously; strain and pour into a sour glass.

White Wine Sazerac

you will need for 1 glass:

1 cube sugar
1 teaspoon Pernod
2 drops Peychaud or
  Angostura bitters

3 ice cubes
3 parts white wine
  (Hock, Muscadet or
  Sauternes)

1 Put the lump of sugar into the base of an old-fashioned glass.
2 Shake the bitters on to the sugar, and add the Pernod.
3 Swirl this along the sides of the glass.
4 Put the ice cubes into the glass and add the wine.
5 Stir gently and serve.

Port and Lemon

you will need for 1 glass:

2–3 ice cubes
1 part lemon juice

1 teaspoon sugar or
  sugar syrup
3 parts port

1 Put the ice cubes into a lowball glass.
2 Pour the lemon juice, sugar and port over the ice.
3 Stir gently and serve.

Uptown

you will need for 1 glass:

4–5 ice cubes
1 part sweet Italian
  vermouth

2 drops Angostura
  bitters
3 parts port
1 slice fresh lemon rind

1 Put the ice cubes into a glass jug.
2 Pour the vermouth, the bitters and the port over the ice.
3 Stir vigorously; strain and pour into a chilled martini glass.
4 Twist the lemon rind over the mixture and drop it in.

Port Squash

you will need for 1 glass:

3 ice cubes	2 parts port
juice 1 fresh lemon	soda water
1 teaspoon sugar	

1 Put the ice cubes into a highball glass.
2 Pour the lemon juice, sugar and port over the ice.
3 Stir gently.
4 Add soda water, stir again and serve.

Port Said

you will need for 1 glass:

4–5 ice cubes	3 parts port
1 part dry French vermouth	1 drop Pernod
	1 slice fresh lemon rind

1 Put the ice cubes into a glass jug.
2 Pour the vermouth and port over the ice.
3 Stir vigorously; strain and pour into a chilled martini glass.
4 Add the Pernod.
5 Twist the lemon rind over it and drop it in.

Grande Dame

you will need for 1 glass:

4–5 ice cubes	1 part vodka
3 parts port	1 slice fresh lemon rind

1 Put the ice cubes into a glass jug.
2 Pour the port and vodka over the ice.
3 Stir vigorously; strain and pour into a chilled martini glass.
4 Twist the lemon rind over the mixture and drop it in.

Last Call

you will need for 1 glass:

4–5 ice cubes	3 parts port
1 part brandy	

1 Put the ice cubes into a glass jug.
2 Pour the brandy and port over the ice.
3 Stir vigorously; strain and pour into a chilled martini glass.

Iberia

you will need for 1 glass:

4–5 ice cubes	3 parts white port
1 part extra dry sherry	1 slice fresh lemon rind

1 Put the ice cubes into a glass jug.
3 Pour the sherry and port over the ice.
3 Stir vigorously; strain and pour into a chilled martini glass.
4 Twist the lemon rind over the mixture and drop it in.

Vieho

you will need for 1 glass:

3 ice cubes	4 drops Pernod
2 drops Angostura bitters	white port

1 Pour the ice cubes into an old-fashioned glass.
2 Pour the bitters, the Pernod and the port over the ice.
3 Stir gently and serve.

Port Rickey

you will need for 1 glass:

4 ice cubes	soda water
juice 2 fresh limes	hull $\frac{1}{2}$ the lime
3 parts port	

1 Put the cubes into a collins glass.
2 Pour the lime juice and port over the ice.
3 Stir gently and top with soda.
4 Drop in the hull of the lime and serve.

Rum and Port

you will need for 1 glass:

3 ice cubes	3 parts white port
1 part white rum	ice water

1 Put the ice cubes into a highball glass.
2 Pour the rum and port over the ice and top with ice water.
3 Stir gently and serve.

Sir Charles

you will need for 1 glass:

3 ice cubes	1 part Curaçao
1 teaspoon sugar or sugar syrup	3 parts port
1 part brandy	1 slice fresh orange

1 Put the ice cubes into a highball glass.
2 Pour the sugar, brandy, Curaçao and port over the ice.
3 Stir gently.
4 Garnish with the orange slice and serve.

Empire

you will need for 1 glass:

3 ice cubes	1 tablespoon
1 teaspoon brandy	Bénédictine
1 tablespoon Curaçao	2 parts port
	Champagne

1 Put the ice cubes into a highball glass.
2 Pour the brandy, Curaçao, Bénédictine over ice and add the port.
3 Stir gently.
4 Top with Champagne and serve.

Champagne Julep

you will need for 1 glass:

1 teaspoon sugar or	4 ice cubes
sugar syrup	Champagne
1 sprig fresh mint	1 slice fresh lemon

1 Put the sugar and mint into a collins glass.
2 Swirl this round, crushing the mint.
3 Put the ice cubes into the glass and fill with Champagne.
4 Garnish with the lemon slice and serve.

Lyons

you will need for 1 glass:

4–5 ice cubes	3 parts red wine (Claret,
1 part dry French	Chianti or Burgundy)
vermouth	1 slice lemon rind

1 Put the ice cubes into a glass jug.
2 Pour the vermouth and wine over the ice.
3 Stir vigorously; strain and pour into a chilled martini glass.
4 Twist the lemon rind over the mixture and drop it in.

Cap Ferrat

you will need for 1 glass:

4–5 ice cubes	3 parts dry red wine
juice 1 fresh lemon	(Burgundy, Chianti
1 teaspoon sugar or	or Claret)
sugar syrup	1 drop Pernod

1 Put the ice cubes into a glass jug.
2 Pour the lemon juice, sugar and wine over the ice.
3 Stir vigorously; strain and pour into a chilled martini glass.
4 Add the Pernod and serve.

Casino Palm Beach

you will need for 1 glass:

4–5 ice cubes	3 parts dry white wine
juice 1 fresh lemon	(Blanc-de-Blanc,
1 part brandy	Chablis or Muscadet)

1 Put the ice cubes into a glass jug.
2 Pour the lemon juice, brandy and wine over the ice.
3 Stir vigorously; strain and pour into a chilled martini glass.

Spanish Cow

you will need for 1 glass:

4–5 ice cubes	3 parts dry red wine
1 part sherry	(Burgundy, Claret,
1 part brandy	Chianti or Vino Tinto)

1 Put the ice cubes into a glass jug.
2 Pour the sherry, brandy and wine over the ice.
3 Stir vigorously; strain and pour into a chilled martini glass.

San Raphael

you will need for 1 glass:

4–5 ice cubes	3 parts white wine
1 part Amer Picon	(Blanc-de-Blanc,
1 part sweet Italian	Chablis, Hock,
vermouth	Muscadet)
	1 slice fresh lemon rind

1 Put the ice cubes into a glass jug.
2 Pour the Amer Picon, vermouth and wine over the ice.
3 Stir vigorously; strain and pour into a chilled martini glass.
4 Twist the lemon rind over the mixture and drop it in.

Ramatouelle

you will need for 1 glass:

3 ice cubes
juice 1 fresh orange
  (or 4 tablespoons
  canned, unsweetened
  juice)

3 parts dry red wine
  (Burgundy, Claret or
  Chianti)
soda water

1 Put the ice cubes into a highball glass.
2 Pour the orange juice and wine over the ice.
3 Stir gently; top with soda water and serve.

Winter Club

you will need for 1 glass:

3–4 ice cubes
juice 1 fresh lemon
1 part brandy

3 parts dry red wine
  (Burgundy, Claret or
  Chianti)
Champagne

1 Put the ice cubes into a glass jug.
2 Pour the lemon juice, brandy and wine over the ice.
3 Stir vigorously and pour without straining into a lowball glass.
4 Top with Champagne; stir once and serve.

Picasso

you will need for 1 glass:

2–3 ice cubes
4 drops Pernod

3 parts red wine
  (Burgundy, Claret or
  Chianti)
soda water

1 Put the ice cubes into a lowball glass.
2 Pour the Pernod over the ice and swirl it around the glass.
3 Add the wine, top with soda water, stir once and serve.

Pale Evening

you will need for 1 glass:

4–5 ice cubes
1 part dry white wine
  (Blanc-de-Blanc,
  Chablis or Muscadet)
1 part dry French
  vermouth

3 parts dry red wine
  (Burgundy, Claret or
  Chianti)
1 slice fresh lemon rind

1 Put the ice cubes into a glass jug.
2 Pour the wines and vermouth over the ice.
3 Stir vigorously; strain and pour into a chilled martini glass.
4 Twist the lemon rind over the mixture and drop it in.

Pick-me-ups

Wherever one goes one learns of sure-fire hangover cures. Usually these are vile tasting concoctions and in truth none of them really works completely. At best they give solace.

Fernet Branca

you will need for 1 glass:

2 ice cubes
1 part Fernet Branca

1 drop Pernod
ice water

1 Put the ice cubes into an old-fashioned glass.
2 Pour the Fernet Branca, Pernod and ice water over the ice cubes.
3 Drink in one gulp without stopping for breath.

Porto Flip

you will need for 1 glass:

4–5 ice cubes
1 egg
1 part thin cream

1 teaspoon
  Bénédictine
3 parts port

1 Put the ice cubes into a cocktail shaker.
2 Pour the egg, cream, Bénédictine and port over the ice.
3 Shake until a frost forms; strain and pour into a sour glass.

Prairie Oyster

you will need for 1 glass:

dash Worcester sauce
1 egg

dash Tabasco sauce
salt and pepper

1 Put all the ingredients into a sour glass, stir and drink in one gulp.

Crimson Cringe

you will need for 1 glass:

2 ice cubes   4 parts gin
1 teaspoon grenadine

1 Put the ice cubes into a lowball glass.
2 Pour the grenadine and gin over the ice.
3 Stir gently and serve.

Flippant Hen

you will need for 1 glass:

1 egg   ½ pint ice cold ale

1 Pour the egg into a highball glass and stir it.
2 Pour in the ale, stir once and drink.

Mommette

you will need for 1 glass:

2 ice cubes   1 teaspoon grenadine
1 part Pernod   1 part ice water
1 teaspoon sugar or
  sugar syrup

1 Put the ice cubes into an old-fashioned glass.
2 Pour the Pernod, sugar, grenadine and water over the ice.
3 Stir gently and drink down at once.

Suissette

you will need for 1 glass:

1 egg   1 part Pernod
2 ice cubes

1 Put the egg into an old-fashioned glass and whip it with a fork.
2 Put the ice cubes in the glass and pour the Pernod over them.
3 Stir the mixture and gulp it down.

Black Velvet

you will need for 1 glass:

1 part stout   1 part Champagne

1 Pour the stout and Champagne into a highball glass and drink it as quickly as possible.

Harry's Pick-me-up

you will need for 1 glass:

4–5 ice cubes   1 part brandy
juice 1 fresh lemon   Champagne
1 teaspoon grenadine

1 Put the ice cubes into a glass jug.
2 Pour the lemon juice, grenadine and brandy over the ice.
3 Stir vigorously; pour without straining into a highball glass.
4 Top with Champagne and serve.

Glossary

Advocaat
A combination, Dutch in origin, of brandy, sugar and eggs

Anisette
An anis-based liqueur found mostly in France

Aquavit
Distilled from grains and flavoured with caraway seed. Best served ice-cold

Bénédictine
Manufactured by a secret process in Fécamp, a most popular after dinner drink, often mixed with brandy

Calisay
A Spanish liqueur made of Spanish brandy, quinine and Peruvian bark

Calvados
A distillation of apples

Cassis
Made of the juice of currants and can be used as a mixer or an aperitif on its own

Chamberyzette
A wild strawberry-flavoured dry vermouth from Switzerland

Chartreuse
Comes in two colours, yellow and green, and is the property of a community of monks in France

Cointreau
Basically a distillation of cognac and orange rind

Crème de Cacao
A thick and sweet liqueur and is the distillation of cocoa beans mixed with brandy

Crème de Menthe
Peppermint liqueur which can be clear or green in colour

Curaçao
Similar to Cointreau but slightly sweeter

Drambuie
A Scotch liqueur flavoured with honey and other ingredients

Forbidden Fruit
A distillation of a mixture of orange, lime, lemon and grapefruit juices combined with brandy

Grand Marnier
Another variant of Cointreau, and like Curaçao, but heavier in texture than either

Grenadine
A flavouring made of the juice of pomegranates

Kümmel
A cummin based distillation. Best served ice-cold

Maraschino
A flavouring made of certain cherries

Parfait d'Amour
A brandy based cordial flavoured with one or several flower essences

Pernod
An absinthe substitute flavoured strongly of anis made like vermouth with a wormwood base

Sugar syrup
1½ pints sugar dissolved in 1 pint boiling water is a good proportion for mixed drinks

Triple Sec
A less sweet version of Curaçao

Vermouth
A distillation of herbs and wormwood

Veille Curé
A very heavily sweetened Chartreuse

Index

Index